RICE UNIVERSITY

SEMICENTENNIAL PUBLICATIONS

Theory
and Practice
in American
Politics

EDITOR

WILLIAM H. NELSON
with the collaboration of FRANCIS L. LOEWENHEIM

CONTRIBUTORS

LAWRENCE H. CHAMBERLAIN

CARL N. DEGLER

FELIX GILBERT

DUMAS MALONE

ALPHEUS THOMAS MASON

ERNEST R. MAY

HANS J. MORGENTHAU

LOUIS MORTON

BENJAMIN F. WRIGHT

Theory and Practice in American Politics

PUBLISHED FOR

WILLIAM MARSH RICE UNIVERSITY

BY

THE UNIVERSITY OF CHICAGO PRESS

Library of Congress Catalog Card Number: 64-15813

THE UNIVERSITY OF CHICAGO PRESS, CHICAGO & LONDON
The University of Toronto Press, Toronto 5, Canada

Preface

THE CHAPTERS in this book were originally presented as nine lectures (several of them in somewhat different form) in a series given at Rice University in 1962 under the general title, "The American Political Tradition: Theory and Practice." The series was made possible by funds provided by Rice University and was held under the direction of the Department of History and Political Science, of which I was at that time chairman. Dr. Francis L. Loewenheim, Associate Professor of History at Rice, first suggested the series, worked closely with me in organizing it, and conducted the student seminar held in connection with it, while I undertook to edit the lectures for publication.

W. H. N.

University of Toronto

Introduction

THE AMERICAN system of government has functioned now for almost two hundred years. Designed to serve a small and isolated agrarian society, it now manages the political life of nearly two hundred million Americans and, in its slightest action, affects the whole of mankind. The constitutional structure of this country has been altered and added to, but it has certainly changed less since the eighteenth century than that of any other modern state. It is still necessary, as most of the following chapters demonstrate, to discuss current American politics in terms of Jefferson, Madison, and Hamilton. If we consider the remarkable continuity of American political forms and then look around at the toppled kingdoms, fallen empires, and transient republics of most of the rest of the world, we must conclude that Americans are conservative in their politics.

This brings us, however, to a familiar paradox: if Americans are conservative, the political tradition they conserve is itself liberal. From its very settlement, America arose out of the dissolution of the old corporate, authoritarian society of Europe. As John Adams observed in 1765, Americans had organized their governments in disdain of the feudal and canon law and had rejected all "dark ribaldry about the divine origin of government." It was already an established liberal society whose independence was formally declared in 1776 and whose constitutional preferences were given clear expression in 1787.

At this point it may be useful to make two obvious, but often neglected, observations about eighteenth-century America: however liberal, it was an old, indeed an ancient, political society and it was thoroughly English. It was old simply because its habits and customs, its language and its laws, its beliefs and prejudices had come with its other furniture from the Old World. Those few institutions of Europe which had not survived the sea passage or had arrived in America in a dying condition were insignificant compared with the vast weight of political baggage which had come across intact. Indeed, if we take a long view, those relics of feudal Europe which did not take root in America were dying also in Europe. It is true, of course, that students of American politics have often used the Enlightenment and the Revolution as convenient starting points for their analyses. When, for example, Tocqueville wrote of American institutions, he treated them as if they were new, isolating and simplifying them, the better to see them, but this was no more than the license of political science; even Tocqueville began, after all, with the township system, "that fruitful germ of free institutions, . . . deeply rooted in the habits of the English; and with it the doctrine of the sovereignty of the people . . . introduced into the bosom of the monarchy of the house of Tudor."

If it is granted that the society of eighteenth-century America was, in all but local residence, old, it follows necessarily that it was English. For it was mainly through English law and the English language, English history and experience, that America derived its European heritage. The ideological arena in which the argument of the Revolution was carried on and in which the Constitution was written was crowded with the issues of seventeenth-century English politics. The concepts of limited government, of the separation of powers, of the rule of law, the attitudes toward a standing army and a church establishment, the right of revolution itself—all these were put forth by Americans in straightforward and familiar English terms. America invoked the ghost of John Hampden against George III.

To acknowledge, indeed to insist upon, America's English heritage does not in the least imply that colonial subservience which America has long since rejected. It is simply that America and modern Britain share much of the same history, some of it perhaps better remembered and acted upon in America than in Britain. It would be the worst and most timid sort of colonialism for America to surrender to Britain the rich inheritance to which America's claims are quite as good as Britain's own.

To claim this inheritance, however, sometimes means to deny purely American origins for American institutions of government. Max Lerner, in *America as a Civilization* (New York, 1957), described six features of American government as "notable contributions to the arts of government." Two of these, the rule of law (though not the technique of judicial review that grew out of it) and the two-party system, could, he acknowledged, have been derived from British experience, as could also ("to a lesser extent") a third—the more recent creation of semi-independent administrative agencies. The other three—the constitutional convention, federalism "as a working equilibrium," and presidential government—he regarded as of American origin. But surely the origins of the constitutional convention are also to be found both in prerevolutionary colonial experience and in the English revolution of the seventeenth century. And the federal system was obviously derived in part from the practical federal relationship in the colonial period between the individual colonies and the imperial government. Even presidential government, at first sight uniquely American, is rooted in the English concept of executive power adopted after the Revolution of 1688 and abandoned in England during the eighteenth century. The real American contribution to politics would seem to lie not in the originality of these features of government but rather in the unique manner in which they were combined and preserved.

One need not reject Frederick Jackson Turner out of hand, or resurrect Herbert Baxter Adams' "germ theory" of the origins of American institutions, in order to find some utility in Adams' concern for the "subtle genealogy" of social institutions and in his awareness of the "ghostly train of progenitors" behind all that seemed most recent and local. The survival of the American Constitution seems a good deal less mysterious if it is regarded not as the creation of a single, rational generation in the eighteenth century but as the slow accretion of many centuries of political experience and reflection on both sides of the Atlantic. The Constitution of 1787 might profitably be regarded as but a modest and visible fragment of a most venerable, pre-existing American constitution, embodied in the common law, in the institutions of local government, in a considerable body of political literature, and in a thousand impulses and restraints of habit and custom. Had the American Constitution been no more than the document produced at Philadelphia, it would long ago have joined in oblivion some dozens of other handsome constitutions written in most of the languages of Europe. It is true, of course, that the style and form of the American constitutional settlement was that of the contemporary Enlightenment, but the relationship between the Enlightenment and eighteenth-century America was, in most respects, more fraternal than filial; both were effects of a vast and gradual transformation of European society. The fathers of the Founding Fathers were not Locke and Montesquieu alone but, among others, Cromwell, Bacon and Coke, Machiavelli, Edward I and Henry II, Thomas Aquinas, and Aristotle.

If we look at the work of the Founding Fathers as representing a fulfilment of earlier practice rather than an abrupt break with it, then the relation between theory and practice in American politics which forms the general theme of this book becomes both more simple and more subtle than it might otherwise appear to be. More simple because, instead of a confrontation between the rigidities of a written constitution and the changing necessities of practical politics, we have a continuum of measured change and adaptation which includes both constitutional theory and political practice. More subtle, because the borders between theory and practice become vague and elusive.

Several advantages result, however, from regarding the American Constitution as an old and commodious structure resting on foundations much more solid and deep than the eighteenth century alone could have provided. The relative ease with which the Constitution has been changed and added to becomes more comprehensible. So does its ability to resist breaking under the many contradictions and tensions of American political life. Students of American politics, from Tocqueville and Bryce to Laski and Lerner, have commented, often wonderingly, on these tensions. The American, it seems, combines a habitual reverence for the Constitution with a marked contempt for politics and politicians; he possesses an inveterate love of equality along with an anxious fear of the consequences of equality; he is nervously fearful of centralized government and yet willing, in time of war or threat of war or economic depression, to accept the most ruthless concentration of governmental power; he combines a stubborn belief in individual liberty with occasionally an almost hysterical fear of nonconformity. Stark as these contradictions are and grave as their effects on American politics can be, they have not yet destroyed the American system of government. Indeed, the Constitution has shown remarkable resilience and tenacity: its component parts, legislative, executive, and judicial, have all survived periods of degradation to resume roles of efficiency and dignity. The federal system itself, apparently shattered a century ago by civil war, survives still.

If one reads Tocqueville's comments on American democracy now, five generations after he made them, the essential relevance of much that he has to say is, of course, striking. If this is testimony to the brilliance of Tocqueville's insights and the soundness of his logic, there is also much in *Democracy in America* whose irrelevance to the present is testimony to the strength of the American system of government. Tocqueville assigned enormous importance to the vitality of local government in America, credited the successes of the Constitution to its rural environment, but worried about the instability and penury of government in America. He speculated on the frustrations of a would-be aristocracy, thought the secession of states could not be prevented by force, and saw no way to reconcile American democracy with a large and permanent military establishment. Above all, of course, he was concerned about the tyranny of majority opinion. To a generation accustomed to the frustration of majority opinion, used to an enormous military establishment, and seldom concerned with frugality in government expenditure, it is clear that government in America has been able to outlive some of its old faults and survive without some of its old virtues.

Similarly, James Bryce's *American Commonwealth*, written a half-century after Tocqueville's reflections, is no less wise and judicious for containing much that is not now of the most central concern. Those problems of women's rights, of corruption in local politics, of amending the Constitution, which quite properly concerned Bryce can no longer interest us in the same way. Even if one comes ahead to the years just after World War II when Harold Laski published his *American Democracy*, it is possible to find the workings of the Constitution criticized in terms that would not now easily come to mind: Laski, for example, regarded the Supreme Court with concern and indignation as an impediment to liberal political and social change. To a remarkable degree the Constitution has confounded its critics.

There is, however, one area in which the American political system failed disastrously once and has had a thousand smaller failures since. A century ago the tension between the slave society of the South and the egalitarian commercial society of the North grew too great to be relieved by the normal workings of constitutional process. The Civil War, it is true, did not destroy the Constitution, but its appalling wastage was a high price to pay for a resolution of the question of sovereignty. Here, it might be observed, is further evidence of the existence, in varying forms in the North and the South, of an unwritten constitution; the constitutional argument preceding the Civil War may be regarded as a desperate attempt, both in the North and the South, to force the visible Constitution into conformity with unwritten but rooted practice. And, in this case, the failure was not that of the Constitution of 1787, but of the older and greater constitution on which it was founded. Neither the institutions of local government, nor the common law, nor the great body of English political experience available to Americans was sufficient to deal peaceably either with the social evil of a captive race, or with the perplexities of two political societies sharing a single allegiance.

The defeat of the South settled the question of federal sovereignty and ended slavery, but it only pointed the way to a just solution of the question of Negro rights. Despite the Fourteenth Amendment, nearly a century of pitifully halting and intermittent effort was to leave the Negro community far short of full citizenship. Now, at last, the fulfilment of Negro citizenship appears to be within reach. It may be no exaggeration to regard such a fulfilment as a test which, in the eyes of the world, the American system of government must pass in order to justify its continuance with honor.

Interwoven, both hopelessly and hopefully, with the question of

Negro rights is that of the South's place in the national society. Whether the South can be reintegrated into the nation on equitable terms, on terms that will allow it to participate in the national life as confidently and fruitfully as in the early years of the Republic, is a question hardly less important than that of Negro citizenship. For the South's reintegration to be based on abject surrender to the social and political values of the North would be an impoverishment for the whole nation.

The place of the South, and the place of the Negro, in American political society, however important, are at least old concerns; in dealing with them the United States has the experience of its whole national history to draw upon. This is not so for a number of grave issues of our time which neither the Founding Fathers nor Tocqueville nor Bryce could have foreseen. How, for example, is a democratic and liberal society to control and maintain an enormous and deadly military establishment as a regular part of the structure of government? How is such a society to be properly consulted about and informed of its government's dangerous and urgent decisions in the making of foreign policy, decisions upon the slightest of which the peace of the world may depend? These questions require fresh and close scrutiny of the workings of the old machinery of American government.

It is the purpose of this book to examine certain aspects of the American political tradition in the light of present circumstance and current scholarship. In particular, the essays that follow seek to illuminate the relationship between constitutional theory and political practice in America, the relationship, that is, between what Americans have believed and put into law about politics, and what they have done and how they act politically. Of the contributors to this book, four are primarily political scientists, while five are primarily historians. That their respective disciplines are still able, however, to approach a common subject in a harmonious and communicable manner should be evident to the reader.

WILLIAM H. NELSON

Contents

FELIX GILBERT

The Eighteenth-Century Background

IN OUR TIME the United States has become a world power. This statement can be heard in any kind of political discussion. It is almost shame-
ful to begin with such a commonplace. And yet every discussion of
American political theory and practice has to start from the fact that
in the twentieth century the United States plays a crucial role in world
politics and that everything that happens on the globe touches our interests. We live in a competitive state system. Undeniably the maintenance of our position depends on the power which we possess. But
the success of our leadership depends also on the impression which our
social and political institutions make on other nations. The feeling of
pride with which we can look upon our history is now necessarily
mixed with doubts about whether our political concepts and institutions
as they have developed in the past are adequate to the new role which
we have assumed or which has been thrown upon us.

Thus our interest in the historical background from which the forms
of our political life have sprung has a twofold aspect: awareness of the
manner in which our political thinking and our political institutions have
developed helps us to understand our way of conducting our affairs;
history explains how politics functions. But in our present situation the
realization of our connection with the past involves, also, the question
whether the legacy of the past is a help or a hindrance in the tasks which
the United States as a world power has to fulfil.

American history has the unique distinction of having a definite beginning. The United States is a product of the eighteenth century. The
North American continent was settled by immigrants who came over
with customs, traditions, and attitudes formed in the past, sometimes
in a very remote past. If the immigrants came in the nineteenth century,
they had to adjust their heritage to a pattern which was created when
the United States was founded. If they reached the New World in the

FELIX GILBERT is Professor at the Institute for Advanced Study at Princeton, New
Jersey.

seventeenth century, their political heritage was absorbed in the political establishment which arose in the War for Independence. The eighteenth century was the decisive period for the formation of an American political outlook and tradition. In the following we will try to outline traces of the imprint which American politics received from its eighteenth-century background.

There is little or no continuity between the concrete political and social issues which concerned the Founding Fathers and those which we encounter in the twentieth century. No military caste, impeding the development of political freedom in the twentieth century, was formed in America as it was in eighteenth-century Prussia. No centralized bureaucratic system subordinating the rest of the country to the capital existed in America as in eighteenth-century France. The American political scene of the eighteenth century was entirely different from that of the United States in the twentieth century. In 1776, there appeared to be little prospect that the thirteen colonies which came to be the United States were destined to dominate the North American continent. With increasing trade over the Atlantic, there was a revival of the belief that "westward the course of empire takes its way." But hardly anyone expected the new empire to arise from the united colonies. Occupying a narrow strip along the Atlantic Coast from the Bay of Fundy in the north to Georgia in the south with settlements in the west just beginning to reach beyond the Allegheny Mountains, the United States was encircled by the great imperial powers of Britain and Spain. Moreover, the internal structure of society did not presage our present way of life. In the eighteenth century there were indeed cities—Boston, New York, Philadelphia, Charleston—and these ports had a merchant aristocracy and numerous representatives of the professional classes—lawyers and physicians—as well as artisans and workers. But the United States was primarily an agrarian country. Although perhaps Jefferson was not entirely realistic, he was not entirely utopian when he envisaged the ideal goal for America: a society of farmers which produced for their own needs and shunned trade with the outside. It is hard to see any connection between eighteenth-century America and the twentieth-century United States, deeply entangled as we are with most areas of the earth by world-encompassing commercial enterprises, economically dependent as we seem to be on giant industries, and worried by the physical problems and social tensions arising from rapidly mushrooming urban centers.

In describing the gulf which separates the United States of today from the young republic of the eighteenth century the question involved in discussing the eighteenth-century background of American politics comes into sharper focus. The relation which exists between the eighteenth century and present-day American politics is purely intellectual. The core of the relation is the imprint which the Enlightenment, the dominating intellectual trend of the eighteenth century, has left on American politics.

Although in eighteenth-century Europe the Enlightenment was only one of various intellectual trends, every important writer felt its impact. Some eighteenth-century thinkers like Diderot and D'Alembert—the editors of the famous *Encyclopédie*—and their close collaborators were protagonists of the entire body of Enlightenment thought; others, like Voltaire, Rousseau, or the Abbé Galiani, were concerned only with particular problems and issues. But all of them were eager to dispel darkness by spreading the light of reason. All took pride in being not obscure metaphysicians but *philosophes* who dispersed practical wisdom and useful knowledge. On the other side of the Atlantic, Enlightenment ideas had even more influence. Franklin and Jefferson were praised all over Europe as true *philosophes* and Enlightenment ideas dominated American intellectual life in the eighteenth century. Moreover, these ideas formed the basis of the thinking of those men who founded the new republic. The Declaration of Independence, the Constitution with its separation of powers, the *Federalist* papers, the Bill of Rights—all are reflections of Enlightenment political thought.

These documents were also an outgrowth of political concepts and attitudes which the immigrants had brought over with them from England when they had settled on the American continent in the seventeenth and eighteenth centuries. The political life which was established in the New World was organized on English patterns. Because of this institutional setting, American politics remained anchored to a liberal practice even when, in later years, settlers from other parts of Europe and with other political experiences increased in number and importance. The British political tradition and the political ideas of the Enlightenment were fused in the eighteenth century.

We are accustomed to regard the British pragmatic approach to politics and the generalizing theories of the *philosophes* as two distinct, even contradictory, trends. But this was not the view in the eighteenth century. The colonists fought against the king of Great Britain because they believed he had become a tyrant. Yet they held to what they regarded as the true principles of English political life, and Enlightenment ideas only confirmed their attitude. Montesquieu and Voltaire had praised English institutions and English freedom; they had characterized these as embodying some or many of the features which a true political order ought to possess. Thus in the minds of eighteenth-century Americans the English tradition could be amalgamated with the political ideas of the Enlightenment and be absorbed by them. In the Declaration of

Rights of 1774, the Continental Congress placed next to each other, as more or less one and the same thing, "the immutable laws of nature" and "the principles of the English constitution." Thus, some principles of a true social organization, if only imperfectly and partially, had been realized in England.

The men of the Enlightenment believed that now the time had come to establish the right political order in all countries, all over the world. They were convinced that they stood at a high point, almost the final point of human development. Morality, reason, interest—these were the crucial concepts on which a perfect society ought to be based. If man pursued his interest guided by reason—and that is what was frequently called "the true interest"—he would become aware that his interest was not in opposition to the interests of other human beings, but in harmony with them; a division of labor would come about, thereby increasing the well-being and prosperity of everyone. All that stood in the way of an individual freely pursuing his true interest was to be removed. This meant the abolition of all restrictions on economic freedom within a state as well as the elimination of the laws and regulations which separated one state from another. The Enlightenment inspired the belief that all men by their possession of reason were equal, that the same laws could be applied to all men, and that, when all men and all nations had been educated to a civilized condition, all men and all nations would live together harmoniously and peacefully in a "world society." It was no accident that the *philosophes* were the first to speak of a "family of nations," and that the term "civilization" entered the vocabulary in the latter half of the eighteenth century.

In the writings of eighteenth-century men of letters there are numerous passages which give expression to this utopian belief that history had ended and that it was possible to establish a society based on the inherent natural laws of social order, thereby uniting all people living on earth. For instance, in 1777, the Scottish historian William Robertson, stimulated by the interest which the events in America had aroused, published a *History of America* and sent a copy to Edmund Burke; in thanking Robertson for this gift, Burke wrote: "I have always thought with you, that we possess at this time very great advantages towards the knowledge of human Nature. We need no longer go to History to trace it in all its stages and periods. History from its comparative youth, is but a poor instructour. . . . But now the Great Map of Mankind is unrolld at once; and there is no state or Gradation of barbarism, and no mode of refinement which we have not at the same instant under our View."

This unpretentious and almost accidental passage in Burke's letter is striking proof of the extent to which eighteenth-century thought was permeated by the belief that a true understanding of human nature had then been attained and that, on the basis of this knowledge, it would be possible by means of education to transform savages into civilized men and to build a world society in which all peoples lived under the same laws. Scarcely one hundred years before the American Revolution, Isaac Newton had demonstrated the wonderful harmony and order of the physical world; the men of the Enlightenment were convinced that the social world was also ruled by immutable and generally applicable laws. This notion is neatly reflected in a statement about Franklin: he "quits the Study of the Laws of Nature, in order to give Laws to new Commonwealths."

Perhaps unconsciously we still hold the view that a perfect social order, fitting for all times and places, can be established. As a kind of documentary proof, each of us carries with him his one-dollar note on which the pyramid constructed by human genius is topped by the all-seeing eye of God and which is inscribed NOVUS ORDO SECLORUM—"the new order of all times." Perhaps, too, we cannot rid ourselves of the notion that the institutions of the young republic were conceived in such perfect wisdom that they have eternal value. It is a fact worth pondering that there is no other country in the world in which a constitution given or made in the eighteenth century is still the law of the land. We may add to, or amend, our constitution but we do not replace it. The most important legacy of the Enlightenment for our way of thinking about politics might be that we feel—more unconsciously perhaps than we openly avow and rationally defend—that there is only one right political order and that this order is the same for all men and all nations of the world.

The Enlightenment not only endowed man with a new feeling of aim and direction; the ideas of the *philosophes* also contained a concrete program of the political reforms and changes which were needed to reach the goal of a perfect society. These concrete demands were formed in direct opposition to the political situation existing in Europe. The idea of establishing a new order implied the overthrow of an old order or of the "old politics"—to use a term of the *philosophes*. The proposals which the *philosophes* presented were patterned by experiences by which they had become particularly aware of the pressure of the *ancien régime*. When the *philosophes* looked around, they saw that they were living in a society controlled by an absolute monarchy supported by the nobility and clergy. The ruler had arbitrary power over his subjects, and the clergy and the nobility had tax-exempt estates. The *ancien régime* was based on this alliance of monarchy, nobility, and clergy. When the *philosophes* appealed to the rights of man and to the idea of humanity, they were protesting against the special rights and privileges of a small ruling group. To the *philosophes* freedom meant freedom of thought and freedom of trade, and that was possible only if economic privileges were abolished. The *philosophes* demanded the institution of a legal code which would prohibit arbitrary decisions and arbitrary imprisonment.

One of the chief justifications for the preservation of the privileges of the nobility and a strictly controlled economic life in the *ancien régime* was provided by the need to maintain an army. Money was required to hire soldiers, factories to supply them, and a nobility to serve as officers. Thus the breaking of the chains by which men were bound presupposed the abandonment of power politics and the elimination of wars. But the *ancien régime* was too firmly rooted in European social institutions and traditions to be overthrown easily or quickly. The political demands of the *philosophes* were adjusted to the needs of the new industrial classes, and only slowly and gradually were they realized in revolutions and struggles which lasted throughout the nineteenth century.

The social world by which the political ideas of the *philosophes* had been patterned did not exist in America. There was no feudal society, no absolutist regime in America, no nobility in possession of privileges which restricted the economic life. In most of the colonies political rights were independent of religious beliefs and church membership. Security of the individual was guaranteed by a system of trial by jury adopted from the English pattern, and a system of representation and franchise assured that the governments were responsive to the interests of the governed. Most of the legislation which the *philosophes* in Europe advocated had become a reality in America at the time when the War for Independence started. It has been rightly said that in America Enlightenment ideas never became instruments of a particular social group, nor did they destroy a social order; what they did was "to complete, formalize, systematize, and symbolize what previously had been only partially realized, confused and disputed matters of fact." Political practice was endowed with a theoretical framework; the prevailing mode of American thought became the "Liberal Tradition." The particular reforms which the *philosophes* propounded (and their philosophy justified) were of little relevance to the conduct of American political affairs.

There is, however, one exception: in one area of politics Enlightenment ideas became a guiding factor in American political practice and that was in the field of foreign policy. Before the colonies separated from Great Britain all matters concerning external relations had been handled by Great Britain. When the United States became an independent nation. an apparatus for the managing of foreign affairs had to be established. Thus the conduct of foreign affairs was a new activity into which the Americans felt they could infuse the spirit of the new times. The Americans entered into foreign affairs with the intention of realizing the Enlightenment concept of a new diplomacy. This was the aim which motivated the actions of the leaders of the young republic; their foreign policy gave the deceptive appearance of being isolationist—to use a term which became popular in later years.

It is true indeed that an isolationist trend seems to have run through all American actions in the field of foreign policy from the first discussions about the possibility of getting foreign help against Great Britain in 1775 to the great pronouncements on foreign affairs by Washington and Jefferson at the end of the eighteenth and the beginning of the nineteenth centuries. In his first remarks on the problems of foreign policy John Adams immediately stated that he wanted no political connections with any European power and that America was looking only for commercial connections. When Adams drafted the treaty which the American commissioners were to propose to the French government, he outlined a purely commercial treaty establishing general principles of free trade between the United States and France. Adams was well aware, of course, that, considering the rules of the prevailing mercantile system, trade between America and France implied a break between Great Britain and France. In the emergencies of the War for Independence, the position of purely commercial connections could not be fully maintained. But as soon as peace had been restored, the Americans tried to return to their original policy. They were anxious to conclude commercial treaties on principles as liberal as possible, but they shied away from any political bond. Even when the League of Armed Neutrality was formed with the purpose of attaining the continuance of trade in times of war—an aim in which the Americans were deeply interested—the United States refused to enter the League because, "although the liberal principles on which the said confederacy was established are conceived to be in general favorable to the interests of nations, and particularly to those of the United States, the true interest of the United States requires that they should be as little as possible entangled in the politics and controversies of European nations."

This idea of non-involvement was reflected also in the manner in which the American diplomatic corps was organized; it was intended to be small and restricted to representation at those courts with which the United States had frequent and important business. Again and again in these early years of the Republic the idea was expressed that diplomatic representation of the United States might be eliminated altogether and the necessary contacts with foreign nations limited to consuls. Thus Washington's "Farewell Address" with its admonition "to steer clear of permanent alliances with any portion of the foreign world," and

Jefferson's warning against "entangling alliances" codified the political practice which the American republic had tried to follow in its foreign policy since the first years of its existence.

The objections to ties with other nations did not mean, however, that the principles on which the United States tried to base its foreign policy were inspired by a desire to withdraw into isolationism. The Americans were quite as much, if not more, guided by their wish to set a pattern for the rest of the world, and they expected that the principles which they had adopted would soon become the general practice in international relations. To the men of the Enlightenment, national rivalries and wars were integral parts of the *ancien régime*, as artificial and unnecessary as the other political institutions of their time. Diplomats seemed to be typical of a political system which ought to be ended. The business of diplomats—the making of treaties and alliances—served only to prepare wars; and concepts which determined diplomatic actions, especially the principle of balance of power, were a particular butt of the *philosophes*. Thus, in shying away from political bonds and in attempting to minimize diplomatic activities, the Americans were trying to carry out a program which had been outlined in the writings of the *philosophes*.

The Americans were in accord with the thinkers of the Enlightenment, not only in this negative demand for an abolition of diplomacy, but also with regard to the positive steps which should be taken to rid the world of its obsolete system of international relations. A tenet of the "new diplomacy," advocated by the *philosophes*, was that permanent peace and harmony would reign on the globe if nations realized that their interests were best served not by taking advantage of one's neighbor but by co-operating with him. The sway of power politics could be terminated by the establishment of free trade. With the removal of the custom barriers, which artificially separated the members of one nation from those of others, a natural division of labor and a harmony of interests among all mankind would develop. Thus the *philosophes* demanded that the only agreements among nations ought to be commercial conventions which would secure a free flow of trade.

It is evident that, as Washington put it, "our detached and distant situation" made Americans particularly receptive to suggestions which posited commerce as the one and only factor in international relations, but the extent to which these prescripts were an integral element of Enlightenment ideas can be seen from the fact that when France overthrew the *ancien régime*, the same approach to foreign policy was adopted there. In the first years of the French Revolution the French also tried to abolish diplomacy and to replace power by commerce. The French attempt to make a new departure in foreign policy was short-lived and ended in failure. No other nation followed the American example. America's revolution had not opened a new era in international relations. Not wanting to live in the "old world," Americans attempted to live as far as possible apart from it. America's "new diplomacy" became a policy of isolation.

The pursuit of such a policy by the United States throughout the nineteenth century became feasible because European and American interests developed in different channels. Nationalism and the Industrial Revolution brought to an end the mercantilist empires of the eighteenth century. The European nations clashed among themselves over new issues, and they became interested in other areas of the world as the markets for their products and as suppliers of raw materials. This shift in European interests away from the Atlantic gave the United States its opportunity. Americans could carry out the advance to the Pacific and realize the dream of an empire rising in the West.

But the separation of the American and the European spheres ended in our century. In our time we are as involved again in European and in world politics as we were in the eighteenth century. Historically we can see the emergence of our present entanglements as a gradual process beginning around the end of the nineteenth century and continuing from then on. But in the public mind, the appearance of the United States on the stage of world politics was sudden, epitomized in the name of Woodrow Wilson. Wilson condemned the ideas of balance of power and alliances because they carried within them the seeds of war. In his Fourteen Points he appealed for a "new diplomacy": "Open covenants, openly arrived at." He demanded freedom of the seas and the removal of restrictions on trade so that all nations could develop freely and according to their potentialities. He wanted to establish the rule of morality in the international world, and he advanced the concept of a League of Nations which would give equal rights to all peoples and which would make any breach of peace a crime.

If one juxtaposes Wilson's ideas and the ideas of the Enlightenment, one must be struck by their similarities. Maynard Keynes, the British economist, indicated in a famous essay that to many people assembled in Paris in 1919 Wilson appeared as a preacher trying to solve the problems of the political world by moral appeals. In the years following Wilson, the United States continued to appear as the protagonist of a policy which relied on the weight of moral appeals and aimed at replacing the use of force by a rule of law. In the negotiations during World War II, Roosevelt, in contrast to Churchill, opposed the creation of spheres of interests in the style of traditional diplomacy, and it should be remembered that Roosevelt introduced "freedom from want" in the Atlantic Charter. Even today the United States is inclined to place particular emphasis on the economic aspects of foreign policy, in the belief that economic improvement will almost automatically solve issues of power politics.

But the ideas which underlay our approach to foreign policy have come under close scrutiny since World War II. A debate has started on the respective values of realism and idealism in foreign policy. For instance, it has been suggested that it would have been better if, instead of formulating our aims in moral terms, which implied the necessity of completely crushing the enemy, we had advocated, in World War I, a peace based on the principle of balance of power. It has been said that by seeing power struggles as a battle between good and evil we aim so high that we lose what is possible. In the final analysis this debate between realism and idealism in foreign policy turns on the legacy of the Enlightenment in the American mind. The Enlightenment tradition emerges as more than a background of American political life; it is still a living reality.

If we want to explain why, in contrast to Europe, the political ideas of the Enlightenment are still a vital force in our political conduct, we can go beyond saying that these were the ideas of the century in which the United States was founded. It must be added that Americans lack certain experiences which Europe had in the nineteenth century and which invalidated some of the assumptions of the Enlightenment. One of these experiences was revolution. As we have seen, in America the Enlightenment rationalized and legitimized an existing situation; in Europe the ideas of the *philosophes* contained a program for the future, and the demands of their program led to the revolutions of the eighteenth and nineteenth centuries.

It is true that to American historians, the United States had its revolutions; one speaks of the Jacksonian Revolution and of the Rooseveltian Revolution. However, the application of the term "revolution" to the reforms and social changes which occurred in the time of Jackson's presidency and under the stewardship of Roosevelt signifies a broadening of the concept of revolution which would hardly be accepted in Europe. There, the attempt to put Enlightenment ideas into practice involved a break with the existing legal order and resulted in efforts to replace it by a new and different one. In Europe, revolution meant the violent overthrow of the existing social and political system. Frequently, revolution was undertaken with the intention of creating a new constitution and legality, but it always meant a break in the continuity of law. Thus the revolutions, which have occurred in all countries of Europe, except Great Britain, have shaken Europe's belief in the immutability of law, while that belief has remained intact in the United States.

Behind the European acceptance of change by force as a principle of historical development stands a view on the nature of the historical process which has remained alien to the American mind. The European political experience seemed to show that history was never final. Revolution was followed by restoration. No social order was completely eliminated and replaced by another; every legal and constitutional system was an amalgamation of new and old forces and represented a precarious compromise easily destroyed by changes in the balance of forces. Thus historicism became an integral element of European political thought. Historicism assumes that all values are dependent upon constantly changing situations, that no order can be final because every order embodies diverse and opposing forces. This view seems to be contradictory to the experience of America which, since the foundation of the United States, has had only one constitution; it is not surprising that historicism has never been fully adopted in America. Whereas the Europeans seem to have become traitors to the legacy of the Enlightenment thinkers, who believed in the permanence of the principles which they enunciated and of the political order which they envisaged, in America the validity of the fundamental assumptions of the Enlightenment has never been successfully challenged.

Thus the identity of intellectual outlook which existed among American and European political thinkers in the eighteenth century began to break up in the nineteenth century. The American view of Europe became equivocal. The European origin of America could not be denied. Europe remained the parent, the master, the teacher, but Europe was also seen as lacking moral fiber and as being old and degenerate. This view of Americans toward Europe has frequently been the subject of American literature. Henry James's Americans possess "innocence," which is better than experience and at the same time inferior to it. But "American innocence" is not only a literary and intellectual problem, it is also a political problem. It deeply colors our attitude to the outside world and especially to Europe. We despise the Machiavellian diplomacy of the Europeans; we are proud of our blunt shirt-sleeve diplomacy, but we also feel that we ought to be as clever as the others and able to beat them at their own game. We are contemptuous of old traditions which seem to have no practical importance, but we admire them. The genesis of this ambivalence lies in the experiences of the eighteenth century. From Europe, Americans had received the message that a new and better world was approaching, that a final era in world history was about to begin. But while we tried to put into practice the doctrines which we had learned from Europe, our masters defected from the path which they had pointed out to us. Despotism arose again in Europe and power politics continued. We considered that Europe deserted its own ideals and our trust became distrust. In our attitude to Europe we have never been quite able to reconcile ourselves to this contrast between admired wisdom and moral defect. One of the burdens which we have carried since the eighteenth century is that we feel superior as well as inferior to the outside world.

To the tasks which we have to face in our present position as a world power we bring advantages and disadvantages. We can claim that we are as well, if not better, prepared for this role than any other nation. To some extent this is due to our geographic situation, but most of all we have been prepared for a position of world leadership by our intellectual tradition: our concern for humanity, our consciousness that the well-being of one nation depends on the well-being of all other nations, and our awareness that we must act in terms of humanity rather than in terms of national egoism. But by the same tradition, we are exposed to the danger of expecting and demanding that other peoples, other nations, other races, must live and think as we do. The hopeful Enlightenment belief that America would arrive on the world scene in the "fullness of time" makes it difficult for us to realize that the process of history is not a short road leading to a happy ending, but that it is a continuing and endless adventure.

NOTE ON SOURCES

Burke's letter to William Robertson, from which a passage is quoted, is printed in *The Correspondence of Edmund Burke*, Vol. III, ed. G. H. Guttridge (Cambridge and Chicago, 1961), pp. 350–52; in the same volume, on p. 228, can be found Burke's remark about Franklin quitting "the Study of the Laws of Nature, in order to give Laws to new Commonwealths." The statement about the Enlightenment as a "completing, formalizing, systematizing, and symbolizing" force in American political life comes from an article by Bernard Bailyn, "Political Experience and Enlightenment Ideas in Eighteenth-Century America," *American Historical Review*, LXVII (1962), 351; Bailyn's entire article is of great importance for the problems under discussion. Likewise this lecture owes much to the book by Louis Hartz, *The Liberal Tradition in America* (New York, 1955); see also the recent discussion of Hartz's thesis in *Comparative Studies in Society and History*, V (1963), 261–84. The remarks in this lecture on the beginnings of American foreign policy are a condensation of the views presented in my book *To the Farewell Address: Ideas of Early American Foreign Policy* (Princeton, 1961). For an outline of the recent debate on the respective values of realism and idealism in foreign policy see Kenneth W. Thompson, *Political Realism and Crisis of World Politics* (Princeton, 1960); for a criticism of Wilson's stress on moral aims in World War I see George F. Kennan, *American Diplomacy, 1900–1950* (Chicago, 1951); on the differences between the "American Revolution" and the "European Revolutions," see now also Hannah Arendt, *On Revolution* (New York, 1963).

DUMAS MALONE

Jefferson, Hamilton, and the Constitution

J EFFERSON AND HAMILTON had much to do with interpreting the Constitution, but little or nothing to do with its framing. Had Jefferson been available, he could hardly have failed to be a delegate from his state to the convention which met in Philadelphia in 1787, but he was then minister of the United States at the court of France; he did not return to his own country, in fact, until after the Constitution had been ratified and put into operation with George Washington as President. Hamilton was a delegate to the Convention from the state of New York, but, since they voted in the Convention by states and he was regularly outvoted by the other New York delegates, he soon withdrew, realizing that he was virtually without influence on the deliberations. From what he said, however, and from what he wrote out for incorporation in the record, we know that he favored a national government so strongly centralized, so consolidated, that it would have had no chance of adoption by the states of the Union if it had been submitted to them. He would have reduced these states to administrative provinces, the governors of which were appointed by the President, who would himself hold office for life; and he would have reduced popular control to a very low point, for he had no confidence in the wisdom of the people. No doubt he would have accepted something less, as of course he had to do, but these views could not command much favor. Since the deliberations of the Convention were secret, they did not need to be made public, which was fortunate for him.

One person who certainly knew about them and, in fact, knew more about these proceedings than anybody else was James Madison, the man who best deserves to be called the father of the Constitution. (Biological figures of speech do not really fit; there were too many fathers.) Not only was he there all the time; he also kept careful notes on the proceedings. These were not published in his own lifetime, but it is safe to say that no man of his generation knew as much about what actually

DUMAS MALONE is Biographer in Residence at the University of Virginia.

went on in the closed meetings in Philadelphia and about what the framers had in mind. His intimate knowledge was fully available to Jefferson after that gentleman returned from France, for these two had no secrets from each other. It is my own guess, however, that Jefferson did not take time to study the written notes carefully, and that he got his impressions chiefly from what Madison told him personally. This must have included some reference to the extreme views which Hamilton had expressed with respect to national consolidation.

Hamilton settled for considerably less in the ratification fight and performed magnificent service in that fight. Madison's service in it was comparable, and these two men co-operated in writing the *Federalist* papers, a work which excited Jefferson's enthusiasm and which has been universally recognized as a classic interpretation of the American governmental system under the Constitution. Since the original purpose of this series of essays was to win votes for ratification, however, and it was written in great haste, both men said some things they afterward regretted. For this reason no doubt both of them were glad that the authorship of the individual essays was not revealed. Since we now know just who wrote what, we can perceive that the constitutional philosophies of the two men were not identical, but it is as indisputable that they stood shoulder to shoulder in this fight as that they afterward diverged.

The explanation of this later divergence most favored by Hamilton's partisans was that it was owing to the sinister influence on Madison of Jefferson, after he came back from France full of wild revolutionary ideas. One difficulty about that fanciful theory is that Madison began to diverge from Hamilton before Jefferson got back on the national scene. Furthermore, in constitutional matters at this stage and perhaps at most times, it is nearer the truth to say that Madison told Jefferson than that Jefferson told Madison. Finally, it may be seriously doubted whether Jefferson brought back from France any important ideas that he did not already have when he went there. A more plausible explanation, it seems to me, is that Madison concluded that Hamilton in office as Secretary of the Treasury was seeking a greater degree of consolidation than he had argued for in the ratification fight, that he was in fact moving toward the sort of government that, as his expressions in the Philadelphia convention showed, he really wanted. This is to oversimplify the matter, however. Economic considerations were involved, and political opinion in Virginia surely was. That is, this was not merely a matter of constitutional theory. Further explanation must be sought in the actualities of the political situation. This episode bears directly on the central theme of this volume, that is, the interrelations of the theoretical and the practical.

Let us now return to Jefferson, who had been relegated to the role of distant observer while he was in France. If the Constitution as framed was a less powerful instrument than Hamilton wanted, it was a more powerful one than Jefferson had expected or thought necessary, and at first glance he feared that it might be made into an instrument of oppression. Unlike Hamilton and Madison, he had seen despotism at first hand in Europe and had recoiled against it. One of his specific objections —of which there were really only two—was to the perpetual re-eligibility of the President, which seemed to leave the way open to the eventual establishment of a monarchy. He had a phobia about kings which now appears to have been unwarranted so far as his own country was concerned, but we must remember that he lived in a world in which kings were the rule and republics the very rare exception. He was determined that in America the clock should not be turned backward, that there should be no resort to the British example, no return to the political system from which the young American republic had so painfully emerged. In that context his talk about kings and monocrats in this period of history does not sound so unrealistic. He continued to be disturbed, throughout this period, by what he described as monocratic tendencies, but his immediate fear that there might be an American king was quieted by the reflection that George Washington would be the first president. Jefferson, who viewed the national hero with a respect bordering on reverence, never thought he would permit himself to be made king. (In passing we may remind ourselves that Washington started the two-term tradition, and that Jefferson confirmed it.)

The second specific objection was not, as some might suppose, that the Constitution went too far in curtailing the powers of the states. He was surprised that the states had yielded so much but was fully aware that their powers had been far too great, and as an official he had had abundant reason to recognize the imperative need of bolstering up the general government. No, his immediate fears were not of what might happen to states; they were of what might happen to individuals. This is a crucial point, I think. A good reason for not putting tags on people is that it is generally impossible to find a perfect fit, but if I had to designate this complicated man of diverse genius by a single term I would call him an individualist. We must remember also that, although in his own commonwealth of Virginia he had observed and been part of a mild government, he had seen nowhere a government which in a positive way could be truly called beneficent. There was nothing remotely suggesting the welfare state, which renders direct services and benefits to its individual citizens. He had insufficient reason to think of government as a positive good. He did not say that government is a necessary evil and I do not believe that his approach to it was as negative as has often been alleged, but unquestionably he believed that all sorts of governments tended to be repressive and that rulers tended to become tyrannical.

In other words, individuals needed to be protected against their rulers, against any rulers. Specifically, the American Constitution needed a bill of rights and he was shocked that it did not have one. His correspondence with Madison on that subject is most interesting and illuminating. It made an impress on Madison, who was himself a staunch friend of human rights but had been giving most of his thought lately to the creation of an effective federal government. It was Madison who introduced the Bill of Rights in the form of amendments to the Constitution in the first Congress. Indeed, the promise of some action of the sort was a virtual condition under which his state and other states ratified the Constitution, and we have always regarded the Bill of Rights as a part of the original document, though it was not actually quite that. (Incidentally, it should be noted that Madison was particularly aware of the criticisms of the Constitution in the ratification fight, and of the explanations and assurances that were then given by its advocates. These bore chiefly on the limitation of centralized authority, and he took them so seriously that perhaps it may be said that he was now prepared to settle for less central power than he had advocated in the Federal Convention.)

Since Jefferson's major objections to the Constitution were met, he accepted it. He would never have assumed the secretaryship of state if he had not. The partisan charge of later years that he was against the Constitution meant nothing more than that in his interpretation of that document he did not agree with Hamilton. He was no anti-federalist in the original meaning of the term, whatever his political enemies might say.

The two men did not disagree on all points, of course, and we must recognize the danger of exaggerating their differences and ignoring the very large area of agreement. They approached constitutional questions from opposite angles, however, and the gap between them widened in the actualities of successive political situations. Had situations been different it is certainly conceivable that the gap would never have become so wide. I regard it as exceedingly unfortunate that it became such a chasm. I am disposed to explain it on the ground of what appears to be virtually a law of history, namely, that excess tends to promote excess, that extremes on one side lead to extremes on the other. To be more specific, I do not believe that Jefferson would have gone as far as he did in interpreting the Constitution in this era if Hamilton had not pressed things so far and so hard, and in the duel with Jefferson which ensued, I regard Hamilton as the aggressor, even though he himself claimed just the opposite.

Some degree of conflict was probably inevitable, however, in view of their antithetical philosophies and incompatible personalities. The temptation to dwell on their personalities must be resisted, for this conflict went much deeper than that. But in this connection Hamilton's personality is of particular importance, because the reaction against his policies and the constitutional interpretation with which he supported them cannot be dissociated from the personal reaction against him. He had constructive talents of the first order and in the realm of government and finance may truly be described as creative. But he was an exceedingly aggressive man, inordinately ambitious, and undeniably arrogant. He was a hard man to like unless one agreed with him completely, and it was easy to believe that he was doing everything possible to increase his own power. He provoked resistance. That he wanted power for himself cannot be doubted, but he also wanted it for the nation. Indeed, that is the best way to describe his central purpose.

Hamilton's patriotism cannot be questioned, but one can ask what he wanted a powerful nation for. He himself gave one of the best answers in something he said later in this decade, at a time when he and his partisans would have liked to enter the international arena on the side of Great Britain and against France. He wrote Rufus King, then our minister in London: "I anticipate with you that this country will, ere long, assume an attitude correspondent with its great destinies—majestic, efficient and operative of great things. A noble career lies before it" (Hamilton to Rufus King, Oct. 2, 1798 [*Works of Alexander Hamilton*, ed. H. C. Lodge (1904), VIII, 511]). He wanted it to play a great and active role in the world, and it is easy to see why Theodore Roosevelt admired him. In the perspective of history it seems that Hamilton's major service was in laying foundations of national power for the future, and for this we should be grateful, since we have had to enter the world arena. In his own time he seized every opportunity to extend the authority of the general government; indeed, he created opportunities. He wanted as much as possible to be done at the center; regarding the state governments as a good deal of a nuisance, he had no concern for state rights; and he was indifferent to, even contemptuous of, the ordinary individual.

His attitude toward ordinary individuals would not commend him to our democratic age, but in certain respects he was a notably prophetic figure. Indeed, he was far ahead of his time. The United States was not ready to play a great role in the world until the era of Theodore Roosevelt, and prior to our own century its major task was to open up its own land and develop its own resources. That sort of thing could not be well directed from the center. Jefferson correctly perceived that at this stage it was of the utmost importance to have local vitality, or, if you will, vitality at the grass roots; and he believed that men will do and dare most if they breathe the air of freedom. It can be argued, therefore, that after Hamilton's great financial measures, which served not only to make the nation solvent but also to widen the authority of the national government, centralization had gone far enough. He envisioned a more spacious governmental edifice than these times required. That was the way Jefferson and Madison felt about it anyway, and if they could not stop him one way they would try another.

They did not do too well when they sought to check him on constitutional grounds in the most important theoretical conflict (outside the field of foreign affairs) in Washington's administration, the one over the first Bank of the United States. In this, Hamilton had much the better of the argument. Here is an excellent example of the impingement of political considerations on constitutional interpretation. Madison and Jefferson opposed the creation of this bank for a good many reasons, including their own ignorance of banking. Their own state had benefited relatively little from Hamilton's financial system, of which he regarded the bank as the crown, and they saw this as another instance of federal encroachment. Madison opposed it in the House on its merits, but he was not at his best in the field of banking, and he fell back on the Constitution. He could find nothing in the Constitution which, in his opinion, empowered Congress to grant a charter to a corporation. The bill was passed nonetheless, but Washington hesitated to sign it, since he rightly had a very high opinion of Madison as an interpreter of the Constitution. He passed it on to the Attorney General, who agreed with Madison, and then to Jefferson. It is from the latter's argument that we generally date the doctrine of strict construction. We might date it from Madison's speech, which contained essentially the same arguments, though they sound stricter in Jefferson's paper.

The doctrine of strict construction is much easier to understand than the one with which Hamilton opposed it. It is simply that a document means just what it says—no more, no less. According to the Constitution the general, or federal, government possesses only specifically enumerated powers, all the others belonging to the states. In none of these enumerated powers is there any reference to granting charters of incorporation. Accordingly one must have recourse to the general expressions—the necessary and proper clause, for example. This Jefferson construed with complete rigidity, as meaning in effect "absolutely necessary." At this point I begin to be somewhat repelled by his argument; it is too rigid; he is imposing too severe a test. And I wonder if he would have taken so stiff and unyielding a position if he had not had so many grounds for wanting to stop Hamilton. As for the general welfare clause, his discussion of that, while somewhat pedantic, makes a lot of sense. If that clause were construed too liberally, Congress could do anything it liked, and there would be no need to have in the Constitution a list of the things it could do. Like Parliament, the legislature would be omnipotent.

The forbidding rigidity he displayed in this argument is not at all like Jefferson when he was discussing science or religion, and does not sound like the man who had said that constitutions should be revised every twenty years or so. But he would stand for no trifling with law while it was still on the books, least of all with a constitution; he regarded basic law as a shield or fence for the protection of human beings against wrong; he distrusted rulers who might interpret law in their own way for their own purposes; and by now he deeply distrusted Hamilton. So he prepared a paper which, though narrow, was utterly logical and which upon its face looked unanswerable.

Hamilton's answer to it is, in my opinion, the greatest paper he ever drew. He had to prove that the Constitution meant more than it explicitly said, that no government could be effective if rigidly confined within a narrow framework, that latitude must be permitted in the interpretation of basic law. He did this by starting with the premise that the federal government has sovereign power within the field allotted to it, and by concluding that in the exercise of this it may reasonably employ any means not specifically prohibited. There is more to his argument than this, but the important thing to remember is that the dominant trend of constitutional interpretation in our country was here anticipated. And whatever else this meant, it surely meant that our constitutional system would not be static but would be allowed to grow and might become dynamic. The essence of the matter Hamilton himself stated in a passage which ought to be quoted more often than it is: "The moment the literal meaning is departed from, there is a chance of error and abuse. And yet an adherence to the letter of its powers would at once arrest the motions of government." If Jefferson's observations of government and of his colleague had not rendered him so distrustful, he might have fitted these words into his own philosophy of progress, for certainly he did not believe in a static society. There is more sweet reasonableness in Hamilton's words, however, than those who differed with him in policy had detected in his public conduct; and they may be pardoned for believing that he was interpreting and would continue to interpret the Constitution to suit himself. They did not give up the fight, and it is well they did not, for he was a man who had to be kept in bounds. He was always likely to overreach himself.

This conflict had been waged behind the scenes, not in public; and there is no reason to suppose that Hamilton's opinion was shown to Jefferson and Madison. They undoubtedly knew his general line, but they did not see his full argument and had no occasion to rebut it. They did not abandon strict construction, though I do not believe that they again used it in a form which was quite this rigid. It was a natural, almost inevitable line for them to take afterward as leaders of the opposition to a government which was exercising powers which they thought unwarranted and regarded as dangerous to human liberty. This was after Washington had relinquished the first office but when Hamilton was more powerful than ever. It was the time of the Alien and Sedition Acts.

(Some extremely interesting constitutional questions, relating to the powers of the House of Representatives with respect to treaties, came up in the long fight over Jay's treaty. Jefferson was then in retirement and Republican policy was determined by Madison, Gallatin, and others in Congress. The episode is an unusually good illustration of the effect of party policy on constitutional positions. Jefferson expressed himself freely on the subject in private, showing himself a complete Republican in this matter and taking a different position from the one he probably would have as Secretary of State. Since this subject is relatively technical, however, I shall not enter into it here.)

The situation created by the notorious Alien and Sedition Acts was far more dangerous to Jefferson's dearest interests than the one in which Hamilton successfully defended the Bank of the United States. That proved to be an excellent institution even though it did relatively little for the agricultural districts. These measures were adopted at a time of hysterical patriotism and fantastic fear of subversive foreign influences (especially French) the like of which our country has rarely seen, though our own generation can perceive a certain similarity to it in the madness we had to live through shortly after World War II, when some excited people saw subversives behind every bush. There was no single public figure in this earlier period of hysteria who can be properly compared to the late Senator Joseph McCarthy, who played a unique role as an inciter of suspicion and hatred, but on the whole I believe that the situation then was considerably worse. There was a concerted campaign, in the name of patriotism, against every form of criticism of the federal government, and against the very existence of political opposition. In short, freedom of opinion and speech was at stake, and the party of which Jefferson was the undisputed leader was threatened with destruction. By silencing its newspapers the party in power sought to deprive it of a voice. This was the policy of the extreme section of the party commonly described as High Federalists. Their acknowledged leader was not John Adams but Hamilton, who was not in office but whose influence was at its height. If I seem to ignore him in discussing this particular matter you may safely assumed that Jefferson and Madison were battling against him, more than against any other man, and that he opposed them on all points.

All I have space for here is the response to this challenge which Jefferson and Madison made in the Kentucky and Virginia Resolutions. These were conceived in no vacuum, and the direction they took, though not necessarily the details, was determined by the actualities of the situation. The three branches of the general government—executive, legislative, and judicial—were united with respect to these detested laws. Hence Jefferson turned to the states because he had nothing else to turn to. He had said very little about the rights of states before he became fearful of Hamiltonian consolidation. Now, under the pressure of circumstances he found intolerable, he took the most extreme position of his entire life with respect to state rights.

The direct part he played in these events was not made public until long years afterward, by which time he had returned to a more moderate position and his own administration as President had been assailed on grounds of state rights by his political opponents. Not until after his retirement was it known that he drafted the Kentucky Resolutions. But they and their companion Virginia Resolutions, which Madison drew, became part of the public record. In later years these documents were often cited by upholders of the state-rights tradition—a tradition which our Southern forefathers naturally clung to as they passed into the minority, but in the name of which they took actions which proved disastrous. Many of these forefathers of ours misinterpreted Jefferson's position. Never again did he emphasize the theory of state rights as he did here, and not even here were these the prime consideration. What he did was to invoke state rights in defense of human rights, as a means and not an end. And it is as a champion of human rights that he should be best remembered.

This question has so many ramifications that I cannot possibly do justice to it in brief compass. For the purposes of the present discussion, I should remind you that the Alien and Sedition Acts have received virtually unanimous condemnation at the bar of history. Therefore, Jefferson was abundantly warranted in inducing the states of Kentucky and Virginia to protest against them. He sought to support his position, as the Republicans had already done in Congress, by arguing that these acts were unconstitutional. Without entering into these arguments I simply make the point that in a dangerous political situation he and his party resorted to the Constitution for defense. Naturally, they followed the line of strict construction and, against what they regarded as an unwarranted assumption of power by the federal government, they talked of the reserved rights of states. In the Kentucky Resolutions of 1798, Jefferson went to the dangerous extreme of asserting the right of a single state to declare unconstitutional an act of Congress which it judged to be in violation of the original compact, and in his draft he said that the nullification of such a law within a state's own borders was proper procedure. This proposal the Kentuckians left out of their first set of resolutions but they used it the next year in a second set which Jefferson did not write.

The South Carolinians resurrected the word "nullification" a generation later in a wholly different situation. They were then opposing a tariff which was obviously disadvantageous to them, but their protest, unlike Jefferson's, was not in the name of the universal human right to freedom. Madison in his resolutions did not claim the right of nullification by a single state. In the final document of this series, his magnificent Report of 1800, he refined away the original excesses and put the Republican party on defensible ground. Without implying that I now agree with everything he said, I can safely say that there is real validity in the doctrine of state rights as presented in this report. With all this Jefferson went along, showing increased moderation as dangers lessened. But the highest wave at the peak of the storm left its mark on the shore.

This episode provides a striking illustration of the intimate connection between constitutional interpretation and political situations. Indeed, we would do well to think of these historic resolutions primarily as political documents. We should certainly remember that Jefferson never attempted to put into practice the extreme theory he advanced at a time when he almost despaired of human liberty and the survival of his party. This was a theoretical matter altogether. It is far more important to remember what he fought against and what he fought for than a particular weapon which he never regarded as anything but a threat and which in fact he afterward discarded.

In dealing briefly with so complicated a subject as this, it is easy to create a confused impression. I hope that one impression at least is clear: namely, that people ought to know more about history. We have no right to expect highly detailed and special knowledge of many people, but surely we can ask that anybody who draws on ancient documents or doctrines to support a position he himself is taking should inform himself of the major circumstances which caused that document or doctrine to come into being. The only thing that can be safely quoted out of context is something that bears upon itself the mark of timelessness and universality. Constitutional interpretations do not do that, even when they are reiterated often enough to become doctrines, even when they harden into dogma. They cannot be divorced from circumstances. It is fortunate that this is so, for no constitution which cannot be adjusted to changing conditions can be expected to survive. One of the major reasons for the long survival and recognized success of our Constitution is that it has proved flexible. Judges have to consider all that has gone before, and they should anticipate as best they can what the future effects of their judgment may be, but, after all, they are addressing themselves to particular cases in specific situations.

In constitutional matters, as in theological, I regard the absolutist spirit as unfortunate. It is presumptuous to think that God is on one side or the other in a constitutional debate. The truth need not lie precisely in the middle, but in major controversies there are generally important conflicting interests which must somehow be reconciled. One of the major tasks of government is to reconcile them. To me it is regrettable that the two eminent men we have been talking about diverged so far, and I dislike the excesses of both, though I do not say that I dislike them equally. I can forgive Jefferson more because I tend to value freedom more than power, to be more fearful of power than of liberty. But if we now had as feeble a national government as he advocated a century and a half ago, our liberties would surely perish. So I must recognize that somehow we must reconcile ourselves to Hamilton. Indeed, I suppose that we have been reconciling the conflicting philosophies of these two men from their day to this as we have found ourselves in a succession of particular situations.

CARL N. DEGLER

The Nineteenth Century

For roughly the first seventy-five years of the nineteenth century, the American people wrestled with two large political questions; not until the last quarter of the century were these questions pushed aside and new ones taken up. The first of these two questions was the nature of that Union which the eighteenth century had bequeathed to the nation; the second was, "Who are to be the participants in the American political process?" At times these two questions became intertwined, notably during the 1860's and 1870's, but essentially they were separate questions and, as events were to show, they were dealt with separately and with different degrees of success.

In point of time the question of the nature of the Union arose earliest. The triumph of the Jeffersonians in the election of 1800, though it hardly amounts to the "revolution" which Jefferson called it, certainly set the pattern for political activity for the twenty-five years which followed. Without interruption, the Jeffersonians dominated the national scene during that quarter of a century, while the Federalists, once the ruling party in the country, steadily declined in strength until they faded away after the War of 1812. The Jeffersonians entered national office with the tradition that the power of the federal government should be held to a minimum, but that precept sometimes proved difficult to live up to when running a government. Thus in 1803, Jefferson, despite the gibes of the New England Federalists and his own belief in a strict interpretation of the Constitution, eagerly accepted the addition of the Louisiana Purchase to the Union. Convinced as he was that a landowning yeomanry was the surest safeguard of his happy republic, Jefferson could not permit his constitutional scruples to stand in the way of an acquisition of territory which seemed to guarantee an agrarian society for the long future.

CARL N. DEGLER is Professor of History at Vassar College.

A portion of this essay has been published in the *Mississippi Valley Historical Review* for June, 1964, in an article entitled "American Political Parties and the Rise of the City: An Interpretation."

Moreover, though the Virginia and Kentucky Resolutions of 1798 and 1799 unquestionably placed the Jeffersonians in the forefront of those who envisaged the states as judges of the Union, the Jeffersonians also harbored within their thought decidedly nationalist tendencies. Madison, for example, had never permitted himself the luxury of thinking that nullification, even of the infamous Alien and Sedition laws, was a constitutional remedy within the system he had labored to erect at Philadelphia in 1787.[1]

During the first twenty years of the century, when the three original Jeffersonians—Jefferson, Madison, and Monroe—occupied the White House, the Madisonian conception of the Union prevailed. Jefferson, when faced with the threat of involvement in the European war, imposed the embargo which, as Henry Adams later wrote,[2] placed more restrictions upon the states and upon individual economic activity than most Federalists had ever contemplated. And after the war, the Jeffersonians in power found their cherished ideal of a limited federal government singularly wanting. It is true that in 1811 when the first Bank of the United States came up for rechartering, the Jeffersonians, by a single vote, turned it down. But in 1816, it was the Jeffersonians who chartered the second Bank and along the same lines as those of the first, against which they had railed so strenuously in 1791. The War of 1812 had taught many Jeffersonians, not least of all Jefferson himself, a number of lessons. It was in the postwar period that Jefferson modified his view that agriculture alone was sufficient for the economic well-being of the Republic. Fearful that dependence upon European manufactures would involve the nation in future wars, Jefferson supported, as did many of his followers, the tariff of 1816—the first frankly protective tariff in American history.

Although the Jeffersonians in the midst of the practical problems of war and peace altered their theories about the nature of the Union, they did not entirely forget the political principles they had enunciated under earlier and different circumstances. In Jefferson's second administration, Albert Gallatin, the Secretary of the Treasury, had espoused national aid to internal improvements as a part of the Jeffersonian contribution to the welding-together of the Union. His famous plan of 1808 never went into effect because of the European war crisis, but internal improvements supported by the national government remained a Jeffersonian ideal through most of this period. In 1817 and after, ardent Jeffersonians of a national bent, of whom John C. Calhoun was one,

---

[1] See his long and detailed letter to Edward Everett, August 28, 1830, in *Writings of James Madison*, ed. Gaillard Hunt (New York: Putnam's Sons, 1910), IX, 383–403.

[2] Henry Adams, *History of the United States of America during the Second Administration of Thomas Jefferson* (New York: Scribner's, 1893), II, 272–74.

sponsored several measures for federal aid to internal improvements. But the bonus bill of 1817 was vetoed by President Madison, and, early in his presidency, Monroe made it clear that he had doubts about the use of federal power in support of internal improvements. Both of these Jeffersonian Presidents believed in the value of such national measures, but their constitutional scruples would not permit the measures to become law without explicit constitutional sanction through amendment. In this respect, it must be said, the Jeffersonians did not simply give in to the exigencies of power, as they had in regard to the acquisition of Louisiana. The Jeffersonian doubts about the constitutionality of federal aid to internal improvements persisted in subsequent years, to receive a kind of final confirmation in the well-known veto by Jackson of the Maysville Road bill in 1830.

During the 1820's the nationalist side of Jeffersonianism reached its high point and began to recede. Several events help to account for the reversal. First in time were the long and acrimonious debates over the admission of Missouri as a slave state. Under the shock of the debates, many Southern Jeffersonians recognized, for the first time, that nationalism might result in threatening slavery in the South. Jefferson called the Northern attempt to bar slavery in Missouri "a firebell in the night," sounding a warning to the Union. During the debates, Southern Jeffersonians turned to strict construction of the Constitution as the surest defense of Southern interests. They were further alarmed in subsequent years by the agitation of the manufacturing interests of the middle Atlantic states for higher tariffs. Long the center of Jeffersonian nationalism, the Southern states, after the passage of the tariff of 1824, began, as Thomas Cooper phrased it, "to calculate the value of the Union."[3] For by that time the Union seemed to be serving the interests of one section at the expense of another. It was in opposition to the tariff of 1824 that Virginians and South Carolinians for the first time advanced the argument that the protective tariff was unconstitutional as well as inexpedient. One after another, Jeffersonian nationalists in the South, like George McDuffie and Robert Hayne, took up state rights as their central principle. Among the last to shift was John C. Calhoun. (In 1817 he had said, "I am no advocate for refined arguments on the Constitution. The instrument was not intended as a thesis for the logician to exercise his ingenuity on. It ought to be construed with plain, good sense. . . .")[4] Meanwhile, in the North, Daniel Webster was also

[3] Quoted in John G. Van Deusen, *Economic Basis of Disunion in South Carolina* (New York: Columbia University Press, 1928), p. 23.

[4] *Works of John C. Calhoun*, ed. Richard K. Crallé (New York: D. Appleton & Co., 1883), II, 192.

following his section's changing sentiments and abandoning his hostility to the tariff to become the new champion of the national authority.

By the close of the decade, slavery, the tariff, and internal improvements were all being viewed sectionally, and the nationalist strand in Jeffersonian thought was being overshadowed, especially in South Carolina and Virginia, by a new insistence on the state-rights doctrine derived from the Virginia and Kentucky Resolutions. In short, the decade of the 1820's was a period when the divergent economic developments of the sections first made clear how weak the ties of national unity actually were. Suddenly the nationalism of the previous two decades dimmed to nothing more than a false dawn, a suggestion rather than a reality. The culminating event of this period was the attempt by South Carolina in 1828 and again in 1832 to defy the national government on the question of the tariff.

The effort of Calhoun and his fellow South Carolinians to define the Union as one of sovereign states was scotched, but not killed, by another Southern heir of Jefferson, Andrew Jackson. In the persons of Jackson and Calhoun the two strands of the Jeffersonian tradition—national unity and state rights—confronted each other. Jackson, in his Proclamation to the People of South Carolina in 1832, followed Madison in enunciating the doctrine of divided sovereignty and the indissolubility of the Union. Scornfully, he rejected Calhoun's contention, allegedly derived from the Virginia and Kentucky Resolutions, that the individual states were sovereign and therefore the competent judges of the constitutionality of federal legislation.

But Jackson's nationalism, like Jefferson's, was limited; once South Carolina's act of nullification had been overthrown, the tendency of Jackson's actions was to diminish rather than to enhance the federal power. In 1830 he vetoed the Maysville bill for internal improvements on narrow constitutional grounds, and in 1832 he killed the Bank of the United States on both constitutional and economic grounds. The Jacksonian policy of having the federal government withdraw as much as possible from aid to the economy was continued by his followers, Van Buren and Polk. Even more than the Jeffersonians, the Jacksonians looked to individual enterprise for the realization of national prosperity.

Politically, the individualism for which the Jacksonians stood expressed itself in an extension of democracy. In office, Jackson carried the Jeffersonian belief in popular rule to new limits by frankly supporting rotation in office. In a free nation of equal citizens, Jackson told the people, anyone could fill the public offices. Jackson's democratic tendencies were also apparent in his conception of the presidential office. He was the first chief executive to declare that the President is the direct representative of the people and no less capable of speaking for them than the Congress. Faith in the people became the hallmark of the Jacksonians. As Van Buren said, "The sober second thought of the people is never wrong." To George Bancroft, Jacksonian theoretician, historian, and politician, "The true political science does indeed venerate the masses. . . . Individuals are of limited sagacity; the common mind is infinite in its experience. . . . Individuals are time-serving; the masses are fearless."⁵ To the austere Jeffersonians, this kind of talk and action was little short of demagoguery, but by the 1830's the common man was an active participant in politics, and the power of the Jacksonians resided in their wide appeal to farmers, western frontiersmen, urban workers, and ordinary citizens everywhere.

The personality of Jackson left its mark on the Jeffersonian tradition, too. A self-made man of little formal education, but of strong convictions, legendary temper, and unlimited self-confidence, Jackson in office transformed the presidency. As the self-proclaimed sole representative of *all* the people, Jackson discarded the precedent that the veto was to be used against only clearly unconstitutional measures. He vetoed bills he simply did not like. As a consequence his vetoes outnumbered those of all his six predecessors combined. Jackson's conception of the veto, despite the opposition of Henry Clay and the Whigs, became the prevailing view thereafter. Jackson also succeeded in placing the cabinet completely under his control, resisting the efforts of Congress to have a say in its functioning.

Indeed, so startling was Jackson's augmentation of the power of the presidency that it almost single-handedly called forth a new party of opposition. The Whig party, which came into existence in the early 1830's, took its name from the proud memories of the Revolution against the alleged executive tyranny of George III. But if in inception the Whigs were opposed to the executive authority of Jackson, they were also exponents of the economic nationalism of the earlier Jeffersonians, from whom many of them derived. Although Northern Whigs like Seward, Greeley, Webster, and Lincoln did not trace their origins so clearly to Jefferson, the most prominent Southern Whig, Henry Clay, was avowedly a follower of the great Virginian. The American system of the Whigs, with its tariff for industry, a home market for farm and industrial goods, internal improvements, and a national bank, failed to be realized because the Jacksonian ideal of minimal government and individual enterprise predominated most of the time between 1830 and 1860. But the nationalist intent of the Whigs was clear, and their economic program, in large part, would be picked up again by the Republican party.

⁵ In *Literary and Historical Miscellanies* (1855), reprinted in Joseph L. Blau (ed.), *Social Theories of Jacksonian Democracy* (New York: Hafner, 1947), pp. 268–69.

The growth of Southern sectionalism during the 1820's, culminating in the nullification crisis of 1832, suggested that the testing of the Union would come over economic issues. But events proved otherwise. One results of the Jacksonian successes at the polls in the 1830's and 1840's was that the tariff and internal improvements all but ceased to inflame sectional antagonisms. It is true that in 1842 the Whigs managed, briefly, to raise the tariff duties, but the dominance thereafter of the Jacksonian Democrats, who were either opposed to, or uninterested in, the tariff, resulted in a steady diminution in the duties and in popular concern. The issue which did test the durability of the Union, though, was clearly a direct outgrowth of the Jeffersonian-Jacksonian interest in territorial expansion.

The acquisition of new territories from Mexico invested the anti-slavery movement with a vigor and popular appeal which, despite almost twenty years of active agitation, the movement seriously lacked. This is not the place to account for the advancing popularity of antislavery sentiment in the North in the 1850's; suffice it to say that after 1848 the issue of slavery in the territories placed the severest strain upon the Union. Indeed, a disruption of the Union over the extension of slavery was only narrowly avoided in 1850 by an elaborate, if makeshift, com-promise between the sections. Like all genuine compromises, that of 1850 really satisfied no one, but it did possess the merit of defining the limits of slavery in all the territories of the Union for the foreseeable future, thereby putting to rest the most formidable challenge to the Union's endurance. But even this advantage was thrown away in 1854 when Senator Stephen A. Douglas of Illinois succeeded in passing his bill to open the territories of Kansas and Nebraska to slavery in contra-vention of the Missouri Compromise.

Douglas, a Democrat from the West, was an ardent Jacksonian, and in at least two respects his actions in 1854 exemplify Jacksonian prin-ciples in practice. Like many of the original Jacksonians, Douglas in the 1850's persisted in believing that slavery was an exaggerated, perhaps a false, and certainly a divisive issue. Contending that the institution was protected by the Constitution, he refused, at least publicly, to see it as wrong. Furthermore, like the Jacksonians, he believed passionately in the sovereignty and wisdom of the people. Thus he sought to solve the thorny question of slavery in the territories by the Jacksonian prin-ciple of leaving the matter to the decision of the people in the territories. Popular sovereignty, he pointed out, was a more democratic principle than the drawing of arbitrary lines, as had been done in the Missouri Compromise.

But for most Americans, whether Northerners or Southerners, slav-ery in the territories was not an issue that could be settled by majority

vote. It trenched too deeply upon values which were beyond compromise. By this time slavery was the South's identifying institution;
to attack it or to limit its extension was to assault the South itself. But
the North was unwilling to accept the extension of slavery as the morally neutral question Douglas proclaimed it to be. Almost immediately
after the passage of the Kansas-Nebraska bill, a new political party
sprang into being, dedicated to opposing the extension of slavery into
the territories. That this new party captured over 40 per cent of the
popular vote in its first presidential election demonstrated the importance the North attached to the limitation on slavery. The Republican
party in the 1850's, it is true, was an assortment of many opinions, but
its opposition to slavery, as Howell Cobb of Georgia said in 1860, was
"the basis of its organization and the bond of its union."[6] Opposition
to slavery held nativists and immigrants, Old Whigs and Free-Soil
Democrats, high-tariff and low-tariff men in a single party.

In asserting that the national government possessed the power to
limit slavery in the territories, the Republicans unquestionably strengthened the central authority. But because opposition to slavery could attract few adherents in that half of the Union which was slaveholding,
the formation of this new, sectional party constituted one of the fateful
steps leading to the Civil War.

The history of the 1850's, which culminated in the secession of the
Southern states in 1861, recorded the most conspicuous failure of the
American political tradition. In any society, but especially in a democracy, politics is the art of compromise. The purpose of the art is to so
balance conflicting interests as to avoid an impasse, on the one hand,
and the total alienation of a powerful interest, on the other. Confronted
by the flinty issue of slavery, the American genius for compromise
faltered and froze. President Buchanan's opinion, expressed in his fourth
Annual Message, that secession was unconstitutional but that preservation of the Union by force was equally contrary to the Constitution,
though scorned today, may well have reflected the attitude of the majority of Americans at the time. Certainly many Northern Democrats
shared his view; perhaps a majority of Southerners did, too, if we accept
the conclusion of modern students of the secession crisis like David M.
Potter.[7] Such paralysis of action was a confession of failure, for it
meant that after seventy-five years of national existence, the American
people were still unable to determine the nature of their own govern-

[6] "Correspondence of Robert Toombs, Alexander H. Stephens, and Howell Cobb," ed.
U. B. Phillips, in American Historical Association, *Annual Report, 1911* (Washington: American Historical Association, 1913), II, 506.

[7] David M. Potter, *Lincoln and His Party in the Secession Crisis* (New Haven: Yale University Press, 1942), pp. 208–11.

ment. Only by war—the classic proof of the failure of politics—could the determination be made.

What does this inability of the American political tradition to handle the issue of slavery tell us about that tradition? Among other things, I believe, it highlights the inadequacies of the Jeffersonian-Jacksonian ideology. If it is true, as David Donald has argued,[8] that the Union split in 1861 because the individualistic democracy of the United States could not stand the social shocks generated by the debates over slavery, then the political tradition which dominated those years must bear some of the responsibility for fostering that fatal individualism.

During the first half of the nineteenth century the institutions which would help to create a sense of national unity were rare in American society. There was no aristocracy, no gentry, no national bench and bar, no civil service, such as more established countries possessed and which would have given structure and cohesion to the nation. Moreover, society was held together by neither an established church nor a predominant one; on the contrary, new sects sprang into existence almost yearly, reinforcing, it is true, the freedom and diversity of American society, but also further atomizing it. The individualism of the Jeffersonian-Jacksonian tradition did nothing to counteract this social disorganization and much to advance it. Over the first half-century, that ideology removed whatever centralizing institutions the protonationalism of the first decades of the Republic had built up. The central bank, for example, gave way to a myriad of uncontrolled small banks; the nationalistic Supreme Court of John Marshall was supplanted by that of Roger Taney, with its encouragement to individual enterprise. By the 1850's, the Jacksonian doctrine of the minimal state had reduced government, on both the national and the state level, to a slighter role in the lives of the citizen than ever before. The few institutions which did command the loyalty of Americans in both sections, like the Baptist and Methodist churches, and the Whig and Democratic parties, had split over the issue of slavery by 1860.

Indeed, in a society so loosely organized, so devoid of structure and preserving institutions, a highly emotional issue like slavery could hardly be contained. Northern antislavery men could push their demands on the South to extreme lengths, while Southern fire-eaters could press theirs to equally opposite extremes. Neither side needed to consider the other. Ultimately the loose, invertebrate society could take the pushing and pulling no longer, and the lifeless constitutional ties, which were all that were left by 1860, snapped.

The war that ensued settled the long-debated and vexing question of

---

[8] David Donald, *Lincoln Reconsidered: Essays in the Civil War Era* (2d ed., enlarged; New York: Vintage Books, 1961), chap. xi.

the nature of the Union. Rather than the creature of the states, the Union which emerged from the war was the superior of the states. The war against the South not only gave birth to a new sense of nationhood, it translated this feeling into amendments to the Constitution.

But the antislavery origins of the war raised other questions which were not so quickly put to rest. By permitting the exigencies of the War for the Union to bring slavery to an end, Lincoln and the Republicans also reopened the second of the large political issues, which, in this first three-quarters of the century, Americans struggled with.

The proper verb is *re*open, since by 1860 the question of who was to be a participant in the American political process was pretty well settled. Both Whigs and Democrats, during the Age of Jackson, had come to accept the idea that all white men, regardless of wealth or social status, should enjoy equality of political participation. In the course of the 1830's and 1840's the last property limitations on popular participation in government were almost completely abandoned, and white manhood suffrage prevailed in the great majority of the states, both North and South. Moreover, in the election of 1840, the Whigs, despite some private distaste, demonstrated that they, as well as the more earthy Democrats, could conduct a successful presidential campaign based upon cider and slogans and appeals to the common man. Then in the 1840's and 1850's, as immigrants from Ireland and Germany poured into the country, the question was raised whether these newcomers could really be accepted as political equals with the native-born. Their clannishness, their poverty, their religion, and their lack of experience with democratic practices were all used to show they were not ready for political equality. For a while in the middle 1850's the Know-Nothings pressed hard and with some success, to bar immigrants from office. But the principal that all white men should be considered politically equal held firm. Never again in the nineteenth century was nativism so popular or so close to success as it was in those years in the 1850's.

The emancipation of the slaves, though, raised anew the question of who was an American. This time the question was posed in a form difficult for most Americans, Northern and Southern alike, to answer in accordance with the traditional principle that each man was the political equal of another. For it is a fact that the black man in America has rarely been accepted as an equal with the white man, politically or in any other way. When the leaders of Radical Reconstruction imposed Negro political equality upon the South in 1867, only a handful of Northern states accepted the principle, and several others had only recently and deliberately rejected Negro political participation. But the egalitarian fervor aroused by a generation of opposition to slavery was powerful enough to move millions of people in the North to accept, at least temporarily, the idea that Negroes should be considered citizens and voters with rights equal to white men. The result was the passage of the Fourteenth and Fifteenth Amendments, operative upon the whole nation as well as the South.

The addition of these two amendments to the Constitution is the most remarkable example of divergence between tradition and theory in all our political history. In effect these two amendments demanded that the Negro be suddenly removed from the position of a political and social pariah to that of an equal with whites. Contrary to their whole previous practice in dealing with the Negro, Americans in the 1860's and 1870's applied the theory of equality of all men to the black man. Furthermore, in order to make the theory work, they used the national power against the states to an extent and to a degree never before conceived of by the most extreme nationalist.

At its best, Radical Reconstruction was an attempt to include the Negro within the meaning of the Jeffersonian dictum that "all men are created equal." In this respect Reconstruction was an extension of the egalitarian movements to which Jefferson and Jackson have given their names. But the sage of Monticello had also been a proponent of states rights, of government locally controlled; in the Jeffersonian lexicon only that government representative of the people and responsive to them could be good government. Thus during Reconstruction two Jeffersonian principles clashed head-on. The root of the Jeffersonian-Jacksonian belief in decentralized government had always been fear of power. By fragmenting power the Jeffersonians hoped to be better able to control it. Radical Reconstruction, if only because it sought to work a social revolution in the South, concentrated power to a degree never known before in America at peace. In less than ten years of trial this departure from the Jeffersonian tradition of local rule proved too much for most Americans to accept. Radical Reconstruction can be said to have come to an end in 1877 because Northerners as well as white Southerners concluded that in a conflict between the value of equality for all men, on the one hand, and the belief in local government, on the other, the latter was to be preferred.

The ending of Reconstruction did not totally remove the Negro from politics in the South, but thereafter the Negro ceased to be a significant force. Moreover, by the end of the century, thanks to the disfranchisement movement in the South, the great majority of Negroes was, once again, outside the main stream of American political life. Although that was a result desired by the white South, the North by the 1880's was perfectly willing to accept the view that the Negro was not capable of fitting into Anglo-Saxon democratic practices. The Republican party, which had brought up the question of the Negro in the first place, professed to be still interested in counting the Negro as an equal, but its deeds in this respect belied its professions. Between 1877 and the opening of the twentieth century, no serious Republican efforts, and certainly no Democratic, were made to support Negro participation in political life, except the abortive "Force bill" of Henry Cabot Lodge in 1890. But that measure was soon killed by Republican leaders in order to insure the passage of the McKinley tariff.

By the opening of the 1880's, then, the two principal political issues of the previous three-quarters of the century were settled. The nature of the Union had been finally determined by war, and the political place of the Negro had been established by a kind of compromise falling far short of the ideal which the Radical Republicans had written into the Constitution. Simply because these two primary questions had been settled, the principal political parties in the years after 1877 found themselves without substantial issues. Consequently, for fifteen years thereafter, the parties virtually alternated in the White House. Hayes is followed by another Republican, it is true, but Garfield is succeeded by Cleveland, a Democrat, who is followed by Harrison, a Republican, and then Cleveland returns. Moreover, the shifts between the two parties in the three elections of the 1880's are achieved by very slight changes in the popular votes and in the party line-up of the states. Indeed, in those three elections only five states changed party allegiance and not all of them at any one time. No other period of comparable length can show such a lack of political verve on the part of the electorate as the years between 1877 and 1892.[9]

One other observation on the politics of these years should be made. Although there were more Republican than Democratic presidents, the fact is that the Republican party was strikingly weak in its popular support. Of the three Republican presidents between 1877 and 1892 only one was elected by a plurality of popular votes and he—Garfield in 1880—received the smallest in the history of the country, fewer than 8,000 votes.[10] The two other Republican presidents (Hayes and Harrison) actually obtained fewer popular votes than their Democratic opponents, gaining the presidency only through victory in the Electoral College. Even in the Northern states, where Republican strength was concentrated, the party's majorities were dangerously narrow. For example, in a Republican stronghold like Pennsylvania, the Republican plurality in 1880, when the party captured both the presidency and the House of Representatives, was only 37,000; that same year in rock-

---

[9] These statements and all others based on voting statistics, unless otherwise specified, are derived from the compilations of W. Dean Burnham, *Presidental Ballots, 1836–1892* (Baltimore: Johns Hopkins Press, 1955), and Edgar Eugene Robinson, *The Presidential Vote, 1896–1932* (Stanford: Stanford University Press, 1934).

[10] Burnham, *Presidential Ballots*, p. 130.

ribbed Republican Ohio, the home state of the party's candidate for president, the Republican plurality was less than 35,000 out of a total vote of 715,000. In the Democratic South, on the other hand, the Republicans constituted no such threat to the Democracy. In 1880, even with Negroes voting, the Democratic plurality in Georgia was 50,000 out of 157,000 votes cast.

Even more convincing evidence of Republican weakness in the nation is to be found in the congressional elections. In the ten Congresses elected between 1874 and 1892, the Democrats held a majority in the House of Representatives in eight.[11]

Republican leaders were well aware of their party's weakness among the electorate. During these same years, as Vincent De Santis has shown,[12] Presidents Hayes, Garfield, Arthur, and Harrison, each in his own way, tried to build a broader-based Republican party in the South in an effort to overcome the party's essentially minority status, but with small success.

With the opening of the 1890's the Republicans as a national party were obviously in trouble. The elections of 1890 and 1892 were disastrous for them. The Democrats made enormous gains in the House in 1890, securing a 125-seat majority. This setback to Republican prospects was followed two years later by the election of a Democratic President and a Democratic House. Thus almost a half-century after its founding and despite its vaunted association with the winning of the War for the Union, the Republican party was no more popularly based than it had been in the 1850's. After all the waving of the bloody shirt during the 1870's and 1880's, the majority of the nation's voters remained staunchly Democratic. The Republicans, as the 1890's opened, seemed destined to recapitulate the history of the Whigs, that is, to serve as merely a convenient alternative to the dominant Democrats.

At that juncture, though, the great wheel of history turned; two years later the prospects of the two parties were completely reversed. The Republicans suddenly emerged as the majority party of the nation, and the Democrats embarked upon a prolonged period of wandering in the political wilderness, unable to win majorities in the House or to elect a President. The turning point is the congressional election of 1894, perhaps the least appreciated of any important election in American history. The transfer of seats from the Democratic to the Republican side of the House in that election was the largest in history; the Democrats lost 113 seats and the Republicans reveled in a majority of 132.

[11] All statements on the strength of the parties in Congress, here and elsewhere in this paper, are derived from U. S. Bureau of the Census, *Historical Statistics of the United States, Colonial Times to 1957* (Washington, D.C.: Government Printing Office, 1960).

[12] Vincent P. De Santis, *Republicans Face the Southern Question: The New Departure Years, 1877–1897* (Baltimore: Johns Hopkins Press, 1959).

Without the ever loyal South, Democratic strength in the House would have been minuscule.

That 1894 was a dividing line in the political history of the nation was confirmed by the Republican victory of 1896. The election of McKinley was the first decisive presidential victory for the Republicans in their party's history, just as the election of 1894 was their first decisive congressional election. Only during Reconstruction, when the South had not been free to register its Democratic proclivities, had the Republicans been able to win substantial victories in presidential and congressional contests. Bryan, it is true, received more votes than any previous candidate, Democratic or Republican, but his large vote was more the result of the excitement of the campaign than a sign of new support for the Democrats. For Bryan's total vote from the Democratic and Populist parties was less than the combined votes for Cleveland and the Populists in 1892. Measured against the margins of defeat in previous elections, Bryan's defeat was crushing; he ran farther behind the winner than any candidate of a major party since Horace Greeley was trounced by Grant in 1872.

Dramatic as the Republican victories of 1894 and 1896 undoubtedly were, their enduring significance lies in the continuance of the trend they began. Not until sixteen years later in the election of 1910 were the large Republican majorities in the House, which had begun in 1894, seriously cut into; not until 1912 was the large popular vote for Republican presidents, which had begun in 1896, reduced. In brief, in the middle 1890's, the Republicans for the first time emerged as the majority party of the nation. The question which immediately arises is: Why?

At the outset we can reject the hypothesis of challenging new leadership. The Republican party in the 1890's was in the hands of men like William McKinley, John Sherman, and Thomas B. Reed. With such men there is no need to look for charismatic personalities or penetrating intellectual appeals as possible explanations for the shift in voter preferences. Nor can we find an explanation in new issues or ideas, for there were none, except for free silver, and the Republicans opposed it. No, we must look further than the party programs and leaders. The only place left is among the voters themselves. It is their attitudes which changed as America passed from an agricultural to an industrial economy.

The significant years of the transition fell in the 1880's. By 1890 the production of manufactured goods surpassed in value those from farms, and some 57 per cent of the working force of the nation was engaged in non-agricultural pursuits. The decade of the 1880's was full of signs of social and economic change. Those were the years when the Knights of Labor reached unheard-of heights of membership, when the American Federation of Labor was formed, and when the number of industrial strikes sharply increased. It was the decade of the frightening Haymarket Riot in Chicago and of unprecedented immigration. No other year in the whole nineteenth century would equal the immigration of 1881 and 1882. Furthermore, those ten years were the seedtime of the city. Between 1880 and 1890 the percentage increase in urban population was greater than in the preceding decade or in any subsequent one. According to the Census of 1890, over one hundred cities of 8,000 or more population had doubled in size in the preceding ten years.

During that decade of transition neither the parties nor the people were prepared by their previous political experience for the problems of the new industrial, urban age. Hence the politics of the 1880's was sterile, uninteresting, and often trivial, as the parties and the voters rehashed stale issues and only reluctantly faced the new. Then, in the early nineties, the decision was made and the commitment of the voters hardened. The question remains: Why did the Republican party, which all along had been sectionally based and numerically weak, rather than the popular Democratic party, emerge from this period of indecision as the party of the nation?

A part of the answer seems to lie in the public image of the two parties. The Republican party was more suited to the needs and character of the new urban, industrial world which was coming to dominate America. The Republicans were the party of energy and change in those years. They inherited from their ante-bellum beginnings as well as from the experience of Reconstruction a tradition which looked to the national authority first and to the states second. The party and its leaders had not hesitated to use the national power in behalf of economic growth by sponsoring measures like the Homestead Act, land grants, and loans to railroad construction and protective tariffs. During the Civil War the Republicans demonstrated their willingness to use the income tax, the inheritance tax, and fiat money when the nation's survival had seemed to require such novel measures. In the 1880's, it was a Republican senator, Henry W. Blair, who sought to employ the national power and treasure in behalf of education, against the opposition of Democrats.[13]

This nationalistic tradition and these specific measures, of course, also added up to a national image of the party which would appeal to urban voters and immigrants. As the self-proclaimed party of prosperity and economic growth, the Republicans could expect to win support from those who manned the rising factories and crowded into the tenements of the cities. Certainly they made the appeal. In 1892 President Harrison told the Congress: "I believe the protective system which has now for something more than thirty years continuously prevailed in our legisla-

[13] See Allen J. Going, "The South and the Blair Education Bill," *Mississippi Valley Historical Review*, XLIV (September, 1957), 267–90.

tion, has been a mighty instrument for the development of our national wealth and a most powerful agency in protecting the homes of our workingmen from the invasion of want. I have felt a most solicitous interest to preserve to our working people rates of wages that would not only give daily bread, but supply a comfortable margin for those home attractions and family comforts and enjoyments without which life is neither comfortable nor sweet."[14] Nor should such appeals be hastily brushed aside as empty rhetoric. Republican claims received substance, if not proof, from the steady rise in real wages during the last three decades of the century.[15]

The Democratic party, on the other hand, appeared just the opposite. It is true that the Democratic party, even more so than the Republican, in this period as at other times, was more a congeries of state organizations than a national party. Certainly in the South and in Northern states like Illinois, there were many Democrats in the nineties who were far from agreement with the national leadership. But even so, of the two parties between 1880 and 1896, the Democrats presented the more conservative face to the electorate. The hallmark of the party under the dominance of Grover Cleveland was economy, which, in practice, meant paring down government assistance to business, opposing veterans' pensions, hoarding the national resources, lowering the tariff, and, in general, stemming the Republican efforts to spur economic growth and to enhance the national power. Besides, ideologically, the Democrats were unsuited to any ventures into the expansion of governmental activities. Still steeped in the Jeffersonian conception of the limited role of the federal government, the national Democrats were less likely than the Republicans to use federal powers in new ways to meet new problems.

The election returns for the 1880's suggest that the Republicans were even then making good on their bid for working-class votes. Today it is axiomatic that the big cities of the country will vote Democratic, but in this period most of the large urban centers outside the South were more likely to be Republican than Democratic. Cities like New York, Boston, and San Francisco, it is true, were usually safely Democratic, but in the three presidential elections of the 1880's a majority of the nation's cities over 50,000 outside the South went Republican. In these three elections, even though in two of them Grover Cleveland polled a larger vote than his Republican opponents, eastern and midwestern cities like Philadelphia, Chicago, Cleveland, Cincinnati, Buffalo, Providence, Milwaukee, Newark, Syracuse, Paterson, and Minneapolis in-

[14] James D. Richardson (ed.), *Messages and Papers of the Presidents* (n.p.: Bureau of National Literature, 1897), pp. 5744-45.

[15] Edward C. Kirkland, *Industry Comes of Age: Business, Labor, and Public Policy, 1860–1897* (New York: Holt, Rinehart & Winston, 1961), p. 402.

variably appeared in the Republican column. In the election of 1884, which was won by the Democrats, the Republicans captured nineteen of the thirty-two non-Southern cities over 50,000. In 1888 the Republicans took twenty-six of the forty-one largest non-Southern cities as listed in the Census of 1890. ·

Furthermore, many of these Republican cities contained substantial proportions of immigrants. Almost 40 per cent of the population of Chicago and Milwaukee was foreign-born in 1890; in Paterson, Cleveland, Buffalo, Pittsburgh, and Providence, over a third of the population were immigrants, and all these cities voted consistently Republican in the three presidential elections of the 1880's.

The tendency for Republicans to do better in Northern cities than Democrats, though, must not be exaggerated. The election of 1892, with its upsurge of Democratic strength in the cities, demonstrated that Republican popularity in the urban centers was neither so overwhelming nor so fixed that the Democrats might not reduce it. Clearly some other force, some other ingredient in the mixture, was operative. That additional factor was the depression of 1893.

The depression of the nineties was an earth-shaker. Not only did it last five years or more, but it was the first economic decline since the United States had made the transition to full-scale industrialism. As a consequence its effects were felt especially in the growing cities and among the working class. A recent historian of the depression has estimated that real earnings for the population dropped 18 per cent between 1892 and 1894.[16] The single year of 1894 saw Coxey's and the other industrial armies on the march, widespread labor unrest, and the Pullman and Chicago railroad strikes.

Since it is true that the Republicans, for all their belief in the national power, would not have taken any stronger measures than the incumbent Democratic administration, the election upset of 1894 might be said to be nothing more than a case of blind, rather than calculated, reprisal against the incumbents. It might be remarked that the Republicans had been chastised in much the same fashion in 1874 when they chanced to be in power at the beginning of a depression. There is one important difference, though. In the election of 1894 there was a third party, and if simple dissent were operating, the Populists should have benefited as much from it as the Republicans. But they did not. Although the total Populist vote in 1894 was higher than in 1892, not a single state that year, John D. Hicks has observed, could any longer be called predominantly Populist.[17] Four Western states, Kansas, Colorado, North Da-

[16] Charles Hoffman, "The Depression of the Nineties," *Journal of Economic History*, XVI (June, 1956), 151.

[17] John D. Hicks, *The Populist Revolt* (Minneapolis: University of Minnesota Press, 1931), p. 338.

kota, and Idaho, all of which had voted Populist in 1892, went Republican in 1894. In a real sense, then, the election was a victory for the Republican party, and not simply a defeat for the Democrats.

If the impact of the depression polarized the voting in a new way, thereby helping to explain the massive shift to the Republicans in the nineties, the activities of the Democrats in 1896 could only confirm the city voters in their belief that the Republican party was the more responsive political instrument. In their convention of 1896 the Democrats hardly noticed the cities at all; they had ears only for the cries of the farmers demanding currency reform. Many Populists, it is true, stood for something more than simply free silver, but the money issue was certainly accepted by Bryan and the vast majority of Democrats as the principal issue of the campaign. Free silver was at best uninteresting to the urban population and, at worst, anathema to them. The adoption of such a monetary policy would be inflationary and therefore contrary to the interests of all urban consumers, whether bankers, petty clerks, or factory workers. Mark Hanna, McKinley's campaign manager, sensed this defect in Bryan's tactics from the outset. Early in the campaign he said about Bryan: "He's talking silver all the time, and that's where we've got him."[18]

And they did have him. The cities, where the industrial workers were concentrated, voted overwhelmingly Republican. Only twelve of the eighty-two cities with a population of 45,000 or more went for Bryan and, at that, seven of the twelve were in the Democratic South and two more were located in silver-producing states. Seven of the seventeen cities in the states which Bryan carried produced a majority for McKinley; on the other hand, only three of the sixty-five cities in states going to McKinley provided a majority for Bryan.[19] Bryan was hopeless in the industrial East; he did not carry a single county in all of New England, and only one in New York, and eleven rural counties in Pennsylvania. He even lost usually Democratic New York City.

Together the elections of 1894 and 1896 mark the emergence of the Republican party as the party of the rising cities. Even a cataclysmic event like the Civil War, in which the Democrats were on the "wrong" side, had not been able to dislodge the Democracy from its favored place in the voters' hearts. But the impact of an industrial-urban society with its new outlook and new electorate had done the trick. It is significant that several cities like San Francisco, Detroit, Indianapolis, Columbus, and St. Paul, which had been Democratic in the 1880's and early 1890's, voted Republican in 1896 and remained Republican, virtually without

[18] Quoted in Harold U. Faulkner, *Politics, Reform and Expansion, 1890–1900* (New York: Harper & Bros., 1959), p. 206.

[19] For these figures on urban voting I am indebted to William Diamond, "Urban and Rural Voting in 1896," *American Historical Review*, XLVI (January, 1941), 281–305.

interruption, until the New Deal once again realigned the voters. None of the large cities which had been Republican in the 1880's and early nineties, on the other hand, changed party affiliation in the years between 1896 and 1932. Also worth noticing is that by and large the states which gave the most new House seats to Republicans in 1894 were the same states which showed the largest number of new Republican counties in 1896. Significantly, most of them were industrial-urban states like Illinois, Pennsylvania, Indiana, Michigan, New Jersey, New York, and Ohio.

To many of us today, the Republican party of the late nineteenth century may look like the political arm of the Standard Oil Trust, but if the election returns are to be given any weight, that is not the way the voters saw it in the nineties. Not only was it the party of respectability, wealth, and the Union, it was also the party of progress, prosperity, and national authority. As such it could and did enlist the support of industrial workers as well as merchants and millionaires. As V. O. Key observed in analyzing the vote in New England in 1896, the Democrats may have got their most consistent support from the poor and the immigrants of the cities, but in 1896 the Republicans gained strength there, too, "just as they did in the silk-stocking wards. . . . They were able to place the blame for unemployment upon the Democrats and to propagate successfully the doctrine that the Republican party was the party of prosperity and the 'full dinner pail.' "[20]

Ideologically, it is true, the Republican party in the nineties had a long way to travel before it would translate its conception of the national power into an instrument for social amelioration. But it is not accidental, it seems to me, that Robert M. La Follette in Wisconsin and Theodore Roosevelt in Washington, who are the best known of the early Progressives, were also Republicans. It is these men, and others like them in the party, who carried on the political revolution of 1894 which had first announced the Republican party as the majority party in the new America of cities and factories.

Hence before the century closed, the Great Republic, which now spanned a continent and stood pre-eminent among the industrial nations of the world, had passed through two revolutions in its political tradition. Through the violence of war the Jeffersonian ideal of the weak federal union had been supplanted by a truly national government. Through the more peaceful but no less profound influence of industrial change, the urban people, whom Jefferson had once likened to sores on the body, had become the new determinants of politics and government. The United States was now ready to enter the twentieth century.

[20] V. O. Key, "A Theory of Critical Elections," *Journal of Politics*, XVII (February, 1955), 15.

LAWRENCE H. CHAMBERLAIN

The Congress and the Presidency

THE RELATIONSHIP between political theory and political practice has long occupied the attention of the political scientist. Nowhere do we find a better laboratory specimen upon which to test hypotheses than in the Constitution of the United States.

The Constitutional Convention, called specifically for the purpose of creating a new government, although ostensibly, for reasons of political strategy, for less extreme measures, was composed of men ideally equipped to undertake the task. Three requisites they had in good measure: a conviction that only a new government would meet the need— halfway measures would not serve; a firsthand personal familiarity with the defects of the existing government; and a firm grounding in the best theoretical writing on government, both modern and classical. The Constitutional Convention, therefore, was confronted with a unique opportunity—that of beginning with a clean canvas, free to follow the dictates of reason enriched by theoretical principle and tempered by an awareness of political realities.

The framers knew what they wished to achieve and what they wanted to avoid; they also knew how to accomplish their objectives through governmental and electoral mechanisms; at least they thought they did. My purpose here is to ascertain how well or how poorly the Founding Fathers wrought—with special reference to the Congress and the presidency. Such an inquiry will necessarily have to raise and offer answers to four questions: With respect to the Congress and the presidency, what did the framers intend? To what extent have their intentions been realized? What explanations in retrospect can be suggested as to the course events have actually taken? Finally, what conclusions can be reached concerning the interaction of ideas and institutions as applied to the American governmental scene viewed in its historical development?

The framers feared legislative tyranny more than executive tyranny,

LAWRENCE H. CHAMBERLAIN is Vice President of Columbia University.

so they set about erecting a system that would impede excessive legislative enthusiasm while encouraging executive action. One has only to compare Article I, the legislative article, with Article II, the executive article, to see how clearly this conscious intent is incorporated in the language. Article I begins: "All legislative powers herein granted shall be vested in a Congress of the United States;" whereas Article II declares: "The executive power shall be vested in a President of the United States of America."

In the one case, the grant is partial, limited; in the other, complete, unqualified. Following the enumeration of things Congress can do, there is another enumeration of things it shall not do; the President's broad, general grant of power is not circumscribed by a single prohibition, express or implied. A further, and in the eyes of the framers perhaps more potent, governor upon legislative freewheeling was the establishment of a second chamber of co-ordinate power. The records of the Philadelphia Convention bear ample testimony to the anticipated restraining function of the Senate, a point which receives even greater emphasis in the *Federalist*.[1] The framers had two objectives: they wished to impede and inhibit precipitous legislative action; they also sought to free and protect the executive from legislative control. They achieved both objectives and in so doing laid the foundation for what many people today regard as one of the most defective features of our governmental mechanism.

Today we judge a legislative system by its functional efficiency, its capacity for enacting desired legislation with a minimum of friction, delay, emasculation. Occasionally we encounter a criticism of Congress for enacting a poor piece of legislation, but more often we condemn it for failing to act. Ironically, in incurring our displeasure for inaction Congress is acting wholly in conformity with the intent and design of the Founding Fathers. In this respect they wrought exceedingly well. If we are disappointed with Congress, we should at least realize that it has not failed us; we have changed our minds; our expectations from government have undergone major modifications.

The second objective of the framers was to protect the executive from legislative control. In their view the success of republican government in an extensive geographic area depended upon the then unanswered question: Could the executive branch of the government be strong

---

[1] Alexander Hamilton, John Jay, James Madison, *The Federalist* (1787–88) (Modern Library ed.; New York: Random House, 1937), Nos. 62, 63. Madison's discussion of the Senate in the *Federalist*, No. 62, makes much of the fact that the framers were drawing heavily upon theoretical principle in introducing the bicameral system. He does, however, admit with refreshing candor that the provision for equal representation in the Senate was "the result, not of theory, but 'of a spirit of amity, and that of mutual deference and concession which the peculiarity of our political situation rendered indispensable.' "

enough and independent enough to provide the necessary stability and power? In the minds of the members of the Constitutional Convention this was the critical question and it was not rhetorical. As colonists they had experienced strong executive power but this experience really did not answer the question they now raised. Under British rule executive power had meant monarchical power, something altogether repugnant. It was only natural, therefore, in the state constitutions adopted after the Declaration of Independence, that the executive power should be sharply reduced and in many states made subordinate to the legislature. The decade or so of governments dominated by the legislature had been sufficient to convince many people, particularly the business leaders and men of property, that only by the restoration of an independent and vigorous executive branch could stability be realized.

If there is a single theme that stands out above all others in the *Federalist*, it is that the most important requisite of the new government is energy. The argument is twofold: the federal government as a whole must have energy; and the key to a federal government with energy is an executive with energy. Both Hamilton and Madison hammered away at this theme.[2] To achieve this objective, the structural separation of executive and legislative branches seemed desirable. By remaining completely free of legislative control the President would escape the risk of having to submit to its dictates; the bogey of legislative tyranny would thus be safely avoided. But at what cost? Complete separation and independence is a two-way street. If the President is independent of Congress, Congress is equally independent of the President. And if the energy of the federal government depends upon the enactment of a positive legislative program initiated by the President, his ability to persuade Congress to enact his program becomes the key to the vitality of our system. Yet the structural guarantees of presidential independence of Congress serve to render Congress independent of him and perpetuate the incipient threat of legislative stalemate that we now recognize to be a chronic condition in our federal government.

To recapitulate briefly then, the framers wanted a strong executive and a weaker legislature; they thought they were designing a governmental framework which would achieve that objective. The Federalists set about translating this idea into actuality in the early years of the new government and it worked according to plan during the administrations of Washington, John Adams, and, for different reasons and in a different way, Thomas Jefferson. Beginning with Madison's administration, however, and continuing with only minor interruptions for approximately one hundred years, the combination of structure, geography, and social psychology served to thwart the hopes and aims of the fram-

[2] *Ibid.*, Nos. 1, 23, 37, 41, 42, 45, 70.

ers. The political developments in nineteenth-century America may have run counter to the calculations of the constitutional planners of 1787, but they have run true to the logical design of the constitutional structure that was brought into being at that time.

In the year 1964, well into the second session of the Eighty-eighth Congress, it is useful to pause briefly and cast our gaze backward to the First Congress which assembled in April, 1789. That First Congress is full of interest for many reasons, but one point is of particular importance for our purposes: it revealed tendencies which are familiar operating characteristics today. During the first session, in the absence of clear directives from the President, Congress assumed the initiative and set about developing basic legislation which would enable the infant government to function. Along with lesser legislation the first session witnessed the approval of the Bill of Rights and the enactment of legislation establishing the departments of State, War, Treasury, and Post Office, and the federal judiciary. The basic statutory foundations of these important agencies remain essentially the same today as they were laid down one hundred and seventy years ago—no small tribute to the wisdom, draftsmanship, and political science of that First Congress. But the central point here is that in the absence of executive initiative, Congress seized the initiative and acted.

Beginning with the second session of that First Congress, the situation had changed. In January, 1790, Alexander Hamilton presented his First Report on the Public Credit to the Congress. This report, the first of four major legislative proposals advanced by Hamilton—not to mention many others in which he participated either directly or indirectly—marked the first appearance of the concept of parliamentary government in our constitutional system. Throughout the five years of Hamilton's service as Secretary of the Treasury, he regarded himself as the President's first minister so far as legislation was concerned, and despite increasing disaffection in Congress on the part of the opposition faction that was in the process of developing into the Republican party, the prevailing pattern of legislative activity bore some resemblance to the present-day British parliamentary system. Congress grumbled but accepted the pattern of executive leadership. There was one significant difference, however. From the beginning Congress insisted upon retaining full liberty to amend executive proposals before enacting them into law. Even in the case of Hamilton's public credit proposals, numerous important amendments came from Congress.

The parliamentary procedures by which Hamilton and his successor, Wolcott, bridged the structural gap between President and Congress from 1790 to 1801 were retained but transformed by Jefferson. Although Jefferson lacked Hamilton's commitment to the concept of executive leadership, he was no less concerned with the practical problem of achieving his governmental objectives. His unchallenged leadership of the Republican party and the absence of any established organizational or procedural traditions within Congress enabled him to dominate the legislative process.

For Jefferson's purposes his methods worked reasonably well. He did not believe in federal intervention in economic matters, hence his legislative aspirations were exceedingly modest. In those matters where legislative co-operation was essential, he did not hesitate to exert strong pressure but he chose to do so by indirection rather than by frontal attack. He was more concerned with ends than means and quite content to perpetuate the fiction of congressional government as long as the end result was satisfactory. The Jeffersonian strategy succeeded in the short run, but in a sense sowed seeds that eventually led to its own destruction. By resorting to behind-the-scenes methods, Jefferson created the illusion of congressional autonomy; the principle of executive leadership lost its clear definition. Furthermore, Jefferson and his chief political lieutenant, Gallatin, encouraged the growth of committee participation in legislation, a step that created and fostered competing power centers within Congress. Had Jefferson availed himself of the opportunity, he could have molded public opinion to understand and accept the principle of executive leadership. His popularity was so great for the first six years of his administration that he might well have laid down and so firmly embedded the foundations of party government under presidential leadership that it would have endured permanently despite the many centrifugal forces which are built into our federal system. He did not do so, probably because he was Thomas Jefferson, and as soon as he was gone, the natural tendencies in his improvised machinery asserted themselves. The mechanism Jefferson had used to control Congress was now used by Congress to control or at least to neutralize the President. The era of congressional government had begun; it was to have two phases: congressional domination of the presidency from 1809 to 1829; congressional-presidential warfare from 1829 until the end of the century.

The period 1809 to 1829 was characterized by two features, one temporary, the other permanent. Interestingly enough, the first of these two features, the Congressional Caucus, had it endured, might have led to another form of parliamentary government within the structural framework of our presidential system. During its brief existence, the Congressional Caucus served to bridge the structural gap between the executive and legislative branches. It may be argued that the Caucus represented the party adaptation of the original non-party mechanism for choosing the President. If it is true that the framers intended and expected that the Electoral College rarely would produce a majority vote for the President and that the House of Representatives would become the effective agency for choosing the President, thus providing a system of congressional election, then the expectations of the framers were upset by the appearance of political parties. As we know, only rarely does the Electoral College fail to produce a majority under a two-party contest. The device of the Congressional Caucus restored congressional influence in presidential elections within a party framework. Although under the Caucus, congressional authority was shifted from the electing to the nominating process, in both instances Congress could not only make itself felt but frequently could achieve its will. It did so for a brief period.

By the time of Andrew Jackson two separate structural developments were taking place simultaneously, one in Washington, the other at the grass roots. The Congressional Caucus had ceased to exist; it had been rendered obsolete by the decentralization of party control—by the shift of the locus of power from Washington to the state capitals. With property qualifications virtually obliterated, the beginnings of a mass electorate confronted the parties with the arduous but potentially highly profitable task of organizing the vote. This had to be done where the vote was located and that meant out in the hinterland, not in Washington. The party organizations lost no time in asserting their power in the single most important area: the selection of the President. Thus it was that a structural change rendered the Congressional Caucus anachronistic.

But Congress did not lose all its power. What it lost in control over the nomination and election of the President it gained in control over the legislative process, and the legislative product. This second development of the period 1809–29 has been less celebrated in our political chronicles than the rise and fall of "King Caucus," but it has been more influential. I refer to the rise and growth of the standing committee system in Congress, both in the House and in the Senate. The standing committee system which has had and continues to have far-reaching influence upon congressional behavior made its appearance during the first decade of the Constitution. A Ways and Means Committee was actually created in the first session of the First Congress but when Hamilton assumed the role of parliamentary chief it ceased to function. In December, 1795, however, after Hamilton's departure the previous January, the Republicans—then in control of the House of Representatives and acting in response to the urging of Albert Gallatin, representative from Pennsylvania—re-established the Committee on Ways and Means, and so laid the foundation of the American system of standing committees. By the end of Monroe's administration, the standing committee system as we know it today was operating in full force. Its implications for the future, however, were not fully understood at that time.

The structural break that brought Andrew Jackson into the presidency established permanently not only the separation between President and Congress but also the divergent and competitive character of their respective trajectories. The President and Congress have alternated in periods or moments of collaboration and conflict. Structurally, no significant changes have occurred since that time; the structural features which have produced the persistent operational characteristics of our national government were all present by 1837 when Jackson left office. They were and are: the federal relationship; the separation of the legislative and executive branches; a popularly elected President; a bicameral Congress with representatives elected from single member districts; differential terms of office for the President, Senate, and House; and standing committees in both the House and the Senate.

At this point I shall shift from history to contemporary conditions.

Recent concern with the presidency has tended to focus on two problems. One strand of comment has centered on the question of whether the presidential office as established by the Constitution and developed by successive presidents is adequate to the demands of modern statecraft. Stated briefly and therefore too simply: Can one man do the job, even with all the assistance which has been or can be made available to him?[3]

The second major line of inquiry has dealt with the question whether the existing constitutional arrangements governing the structure of the Congress and the relationship between the President and Congress are adequate. An assumption, either explicit or implicit, underlying this question is that if the President is able to have his way with Congress, to persuade Congress to accept his proposals, then the relationship is adequate.[4]

It may be noted in passing that a third possible problem—the potential danger of presidential dictatorship—does not at present attract very much attention. Ironically, it was this aspect of our constitutional system that aroused concern and inspired most of the polemical writing in the

---

[3] Two recent works emphasizing this aspect of the problem are Herman Finer, *The Presidency* (Chicago: University of Chicago Press, 1960), and Rexford G. Tugwell, *The Enlargement of the Presidency* (Garden City, N.Y.: Doubleday, 1960).

[4] This theme has been emphasized in most of the literature on the presidency of the past decade. A recent succinct statement of this viewpoint is James M. Burns, "Excellence and Leadership in President and Congress," *Daedalus: Journal of the American Academy of Arts and Sciences*, Fall, 1961, pp. 734–49. For a more comprehensive presentation of this theme see the same author's *Roosevelt: The Lion and the Fox* (New York: Harcourt, Brace, 1956), chaps. 14, 18, and the Appendix.

last decades of the nineteenth century.[5] Some recent American writers, notably Edward S. Corwin and C. Perry Patterson,[6] have warned of the dangers of presidential aggrandizement, but their voices have been all but drowned by the swelling chorus which carries the other two themes.

I shall not attempt to stretch limited space to deal with both the issues indicated above. The question of presidential adequacy—whether a single individual can discharge responsibly the manifold duties of his office—I leave to someone else or to another occasion, except for a single observation. Under modern conditions, the one obligation a President cannot escape is a clear, sharp-edged conception of the indispensable function of his office: the role which he and he alone can discharge if his presidency is to fulfil its constitutional mandate. To state the problem is not to solve it, but the issue is reasonably clear. Much of the work of the presidential office need not and should not occupy the President. The decision of what should occupy him is less that of an efficiency expert or a job analyst than that of the President himself as he faces the question which is both personal and political: What for me is the "indispensable function"? Depending upon his own personality, work habits, special interests, and capabilities—not to mention the time and events in which he serves—each President must seek and find his own answer to this question. The extent to which he forces himself to find the answer, and once having found it to abide by it, will determine whether, for his administration, the job is too big for the man.[7]

II

My purpose for the remainder of this paper is to examine the congressional-presidential relationship as it is today. Specifically, how have the factors already noted operated under current conditions? Time does not permit even a brief summary of political developments since 1837, but it is sufficient to say that in general the doctrine of presidential leadership in legislation is a twentieth-century phenomenon. The attempt by the President to persuade the Congress to share its legislative responsibilities, coming late as it did, left Congress free during most of the nineteenth century to develop and solidify its own particular legislative

[5] Adolphe de Chambrun, *The Executive Power in the United States*, trans. Madeleine Vinton Dahlgren (Lancaster, Pa.: Inquirer Printing and Publishing Co., 1874); Henry C. Lockwood, *The Abolition of the Presidency* (New York: R. Worthington, 1884).

[6] Edward S. Corwin, *The President: Office and Powers* (New York: New York University Press, 1948); C. Perry Patterson, *Presidential Government in the United States* (Chapel Hill: University of North Carolina Press, 1947).

[7] For a somewhat different emphasis concerning the basic issue of presidential effectiveness, see Richard E. Neustadt, *Presidential Power* (New York: John Wiley & Sons, 1960). I share Mr. Neustadt's view, but feel that considered in its broadest terms, the issue of presidential power cannot be separated from the central question of selective emphasis—the indispensable function.

procedures and traditions. This must be taken into account in considering the developments of the past sixty years.

At this time we have a Democratic President and heavy Democratic majorities in the House of Representatives and Senate. To a foreign observer this would seem to assure that any decisions made by President Johnson concerning necessary legislation could be readily effectuated. To any American the problem is not that simple, although the exact reasons are not always clear. One of the central issues today, so far as the national government is concerned, is concentrated in the meaning of presidential leadership. If there is a single difference in presidential-congressional relationships between the twentieth century and earlier, I think it is the general agreement today upon the necessity and desirability of presidential leadership. We do not always define our conception of that term, but by and large I would say it includes leadership in legislation as well as in other aspects of the nation's life. We may not agree with the President's legislative proposals; indeed some will be likely to disagree with almost all of them. Nevertheless, whether we favor or oppose his specific recommendations, we tend to believe that he should speak out; this is a responsibility that he has obligated himself to discharge by accepting the post of President.

As I have said, this attitude toward presidential leadership, particularly in the area of legislation, is primarily a twentieth-century phenomenon. Just how it came about and the various factors that contributed to it need not be dwelt on here. It is enough to say that the idea has been evolutionary and cumulative; if it was tentative and controversial a half-century ago, that is no longer true. Even Congress, the one institution that might be expected to voice a dissenting note, is in general agreement with the proposition that the President should not abdicate his constitutional responsibility for recommending legislation.

It is precisely at this point that a difference of opinion between what I shall call the presidential view and the congressional view occurs. The congressional view distinguishes between presidential leadership in the form of recommendations and presidential leadership that extends beyond this step. Furthermore, according to the congressional view, the President does not and should not enjoy a monopoly in recommending legislation. Congress, being a co-ordinate branch of the government, considers that its function embraces all aspects of the legislative process including that of initiation; it is willing to share the function of proposing legislation but not to relinquish it; it is willing to receive presidential recommendations, to consider them, but not to admit that they enjoy or should be accorded special status. It goes without saying that Walter Lippmann does not represent the congressional view when he asserts, "The executive is the active power in the state, the asking and the proposing power. The representative assembly is the consenting power, the petitioning, the approving and the criticizing, the accepting and refusing power."[8] Much of Lippmann's formula is acceptable in the congressional view, but it imposes boundaries that are too restrictive.

The evidence that there is a real and fundamental difference between the presidential and congressional views concerning legislative leadership is to be found both in what Congress does and what it says. Presidential legislative programs get whacked, hacked, and derailed more often than they get approved. This has been true regardless of party, so it must be attributed to something other than party politics. But we have more direct testimony concerning the congressional view.

It may be recalled that Congress passed the Legislative Reorganization Act in 1946. This was the first comprehensive congressional reorganization in the history of the country. It was preceded by extensive hearings, and much of the testimony was provided by congressmen themselves; so there was an excellent opportunity to ascertain the congressional view. In the thousand pages of testimony accumulated by the joint House-Senate committee one gets the unmistakable impression that to its members congressional reform meant congressional reassertion of its responsibility as the legislative branch under the Constitution. It would be wrong to assume that the chief forces behind this congressional resurgence were anti-administration congressmen who sought in this way to block legislative policies which they disliked. Some of the staunchest supporters of the New Deal program were among the most active advocates of strengthening Congress. To this group—and there is reason to believe they reflected the opinion of the overwhelming majority of congressmen without reference to party or chamber—congressional reorganization had become imperative because it provided the only way in which Congress could recoup that which it had lost—the dominant role in legislation. In his testimony before the joint committee, Representative Jerry Voorhis stated succinctly the thought that can be found running through all the hearings:

The Congress of the United States holds within its own hands the determination of its own future and hence the future of our American Government itself. For one possible course of development would consist of a continuous extension of the power and authority of the executive branch of government, the abandonment by Congress to the executive department of the admittedly difficult and detailed job of conceiving precise legislation to meet the needs and problems of modern America, and the reduction of the Congress to the position of a mere ratifying body, either approving or disapproving Executive acts and proposals and occasionally making broad and indeterminate grants of power to the Executive.

[8] Walter Lippmann, *Essays in the Public Philosophy* (Boston: Little, Brown, 1955), p. 30.

I doubt that more than a mere handful of Americans would consciously favor such a course for our country's Government. It means the gradual growth of a type of government which the whole tradition of our country is against.[9]

I think Mr. Voorhis has interpreted the congressional position accurately. His statement concerning the public in general may occasion some debate, but I think that, here too, he expresses the congressional view. It may be well to consider for a moment the elusive issue of public opinion toward Congress. It frequently appears that the "public" is impatient with Congress. This is the "visible public," represented by editorial writers, columnists, groups seeking certain action—frequently "liberal" groups—political scientists offended by illogical or irrational procedures, and by persons or groups who feel that our national integrity is being jeopardized by irresponsible politicians.

But there are other "publics": those who are happy that offensive legislation has been prevented; those who are doctrinally Whig or who believe in laissez faire or state rights; those in each constituency who for one reason or another support their congressman who espouses the anti-administration or at least the independent Congress view. There are the congressmen themselves and their individual or collective image of themselves as they believe they appear to the outside world. At any particular moment, when a crucial issue comes up for decision, the climate of opinion within each chamber may be more important than that in the outside world. Were Congress to recess or suspend action by some other procedure and thus afford individual members an opportunity to recheck their political bearings they might change their vote, but in the absence of this the psychology of their chamber may be contagious enough to determine their vote. Causal factors underlying congressional behavior are exceedingly complex; the foregoing discussion is intended as illustrative only; no attempt is made to be complete. The point I wish to emphasize is: Congress itself does not share or accept the rather unfavorable image that is frequently projected by its most articulate critics. Unless this fact is kept in mind, it is impossible to see the issue of presidential-congressional relationships in clear perspective.

Let us then take a brief look at the personnel of Congress, the world in which they live, the factors which affect their work, their attitudes, their performance. First, a word about the general quality of men who today make up Congress. There are few informed and unprejudiced observers who would subscribe to the opinion expressed by Tocqueville a century and a quarter ago, when he wrote:

[9] *Hearings before the Joint Committee on the Organization of Congress*, 79 Cong., 1 sess., March 19, 1945, p. 24.

In the United States those who engage in the perplexities of political life are persons of very moderate pretensions. The pursuit of wealth generally diverts men of great talents and strong passions from the pursuit of power; and it frequently happens that a man does not undertake to direct the affairs of the state until he has shown himself incompetent to conduct his own. The vast number of very ordinary men who occupy the public stations is quite as attributable to these causes as to the bad choice of democracy. In the United States I am not sure that the people would choose men of superior abilities even if they wished to be elected; but it is certain that candidates of this description do not come forward.[10]

Whatever the reasons, the situation Tocqueville purported to describe is not an accurate description of conditions prevailing today. Not all men who serve in Congress today are persons of wisdom and ability, but I think it can be said that the quality of person in public service, including Congress, compares favorably with that in other lines of endeavor. The question then is whether considerations other than ability affect the individual performance of the congressman and color his behavior.

Here also Tocqueville has expressed a view and I think that in this instance he is correct.[11] He observes that in aristocratic countries, members of the legislature, being aristocrats themselves—hence already men of prominence—look upon their position in the legislature as less important than their position in the country. By contrast, in democratic countries, particularly the United States, the legislator considers his position in the legislature more important than his position in the country. His official status, in other words, is greater than his private status; as a congressman he enjoys prestige that he could not claim as a private citizen. In Tocqueville's view, and I think he is right, there is a direct connection between the individual congressman's pride of office and his concern for the one and only entity that governs his fate: his constituency. Unless he can continue to please his constituents, he is an ex-congressman very quickly. So long as he can satisfy his constituents or enough of them to assure re-election, he is invulnerable—to party, to congressional leaders, to the President. The real essence of congressional independence lies in this fact. All talk about party responsibility, party discipline, party government remains just talk if this central fact of life is ignored.[12]

[10] Alexis de Tocqueville, *Democracy in America*, ed. Phillips Bradley (2 vols.; New York: Alfred A. Knopf, 1945), I, 208.

[11] *Ibid.*, II, 90.

[12] Although the dominance of the President in our national legislative program is also a fact of life apparent to all, he has no structural resources to which he can resort when his personal or party appeal is not strong enough to assure him victory. When the congressional

The constituency orientation of the congressman, be he senator or representative, is one salient factor in congressional behavior; the urgency of political survival gives constituency a primacy unequaled by any other single consideration. Most of the time of the congressman, once he is elected, however, is spent not in his constituency but in Washington.[13] His working relationships constitute the second major influence in his behavior. Between these two, constituency and chamber, are to be found most of the effective causes of congressional decision-making.[14] At different times priority may shift from one to the other. The approach of elections understandably pushes constituency to the fore. Whether at this period the individual congressman will draw close to the President depends upon his reading of the political barometer. So far as his day-by-day existence in Washington is concerned, his single most continuous and intensive association will be with the committee or committees on which he serves.

The rapid growth of the standing committee system is a strong indication of its appeal to the congressional spirit or what one might term the American legislative instinct.[15] The political theorist has not yet seen fit to direct his attention to the phenomenon of the American standing committee although the student of social structure will find much of interest here.[16] At this point it is possible to offer only a few observa-

---

horse does not respond to his verbal directions, he has a small switch in the form of rather inconsequential patronage but he has no bridle and bit by which he can add physical force to his verbal exhortations.

[13] Exceptions to this statement occur chiefly in the case of a few congressmen, mostly representatives, who because they live in nearby metropolitan areas discharge their congressional obligations on a commuting basis. These individuals fall outside the normal mode; they do not make enough impact to alter the general pattern of behavior.

[14] But see David B. Truman, *The Congressional Party* (New York: John Wiley & Sons, 1959), pp. 249 ff. Professor Truman stresses the importance of the state delegation (the collective group of congressmen of the same political party from a particular state) in his catalogue of factors which influence individual decision-making. The possible impact of this group is not challenged; whether the state delegation or the standing committee will be most influential will depend primarily upon the subject at issue.

[15] One can search in vain for early awareness of the imminence of standing committees. The subject does not seem to have occupied the attention of the Founding Fathers. The *Federalist* essays are equally barren. Except in Virginia and Pennsylvania permanent standing committees had not been a regular feature of legislative activity either in the colonial or state legislatures. Little use of standing committees in the modern sense was made by the Continental Congresses. The standing committee was, in fact, a British import rather than an indigenous institution, but its English history bore little resemblance to its exuberant growth in the national Congress.

[16] Aside from the pioneering volume by Lauros G. McConachie, *Congressional Committees* (New York: T. Y. Crowell, 1898), a book still very much worth reading despite the author's rather ambiguous style, no major work on the standing committee system exists. Nor have the numerous writers on Congress devoted more than passing attention to this unique feature of our government. Despite Woodrow Wilson's much quoted comment that ours is "a

tions, but no theory of political institutions will have full relevance for the American political scene until the operational realities of the committee system are included. The average congressman looks for more than job security. He seeks recognition, respect, a sense of importance. This can be achieved only if he believes that his job is important, that his organization is essential, and that his role in it is vital. This positive, constructive factor has been supplied by the standing committees. They appeared and have prospered because they met a fundamental psychological and sociological need. So long as that need continues to exist no amount of exhortation is likely to persuade congressmen to immolate themselves because the committee system prevents concerted action, hence unified programmatic behavior by Congress as a whole. To the individual congressman this argument is beside the point.

For most members of Congress, the available career opportunities lie in the realm of committee preferment rather than in the chamber as a whole. The likelihood of achieving one of the half-dozen positions comprising the House and Senate leadership is considerable for only a handful of the more than five hundred individuals who make up the Congress at any given moment. The odds are much better for them when they survey the opportunities for recognition in the two dozen major standing committees. Each member will serve on one or more committees. If he is fortunate, he will usually land—if not at first, before too long—on a committee which deals with legislation of interest to important groups within his own constituency, so his efforts will not be wholly unrelated to the practical problem of political survival. Given time and staying power, a member can hope for ultimate success: chairmanship of a standing committee. There are lesser and more immediate rewards, however, that the standing committee system affords even the new—and possibly temporary—member; indeed, they may be important factors in enabling him to consolidate his electoral strength and prolong his sojourn in Washington.

Committee membership gives the able, energetic, and ambitious newcomer a chance to establish his identity and demonstrate his claim to recognition. The committee is a small enough unit for individual capacities to become quickly visible. There is also sufficient division of labor so that the efficient and conscientious member can soon establish some competence and eventually real expertness in the subject matter of his committee. Equivalent avenues of cultivation on the personnel side are exploitable. Through his committee contacts the member can quickly become acquainted with the key people in the administration and bu-

government by the Standing Committees of Congress," he does not attempt to explain the origin of these committees or the factors which have made them so important. The quotation appears in *Congressional Government* (1885; New York: Meridian Books, 1956), p. 56.

reaucracy who deal in the subject matter of his committee. Finally, and by no means least important, he will find that with very little effort on his own part he has become an important person in the eyes of the interest groups whose hopes and fears center in the decisions on public policy that his committee makes.

It is no exaggeration to say that from the inside view the life, hope, success, loyalty, and personal identification of the average congressman is more closely tied up with the committee than with the chamber or the Congress. The larger identification is never wholly absent and the individual member can at times be influenced by appeals that focus upon his constitutional status. Furthermore, like every other politician, he cannot ignore the factors of party, presidential influence, and crisis. All these are at least one step removed from the day-by-day facts of existence, however. They do not have continuous operational force. In many situations they will simply not be articulated clearly enough to provide the legislator with any guidance whatsoever, so he must look elsewhere for his cues. Having developed a sense of direction, and along with it a basic orientation to the segment of public policy over which he and his committee colleagues stand guard, he may be little inclined to alter course even when the signal from external agencies is clear, definite, and urgent.

Congress is basically feudal. No baron out of the twelfth century was ever more conscious of his domain, his prerogatives, and his independence from central control than is the standing committee chairman. Two elements are present here. The committee itself has a strong sense of autonomy. Its chairman embodies both the collective egocentricity of the committee and his own personal *amour-propre*. In general, the committee chairman has reached the apex of his career—but also the end of the line. There is nowhere else he can go. He is no longer on the make; therefore, he is not as likely to be interested in new ideas, new propositions, new worlds to conquer, as he is in consolidating his power and entrenching his position. The politics of the President, the party, or even Congress are not necessarily the politics of the committee chairman in either chamber. His preferences or antipathies may stem from partisan alignments, but they may be more directly and intimately inspired by such non-partisan factors as economic, sectional, religious, or philosophical stimuli. Underlying or overshadowing all these are more strictly personal considerations of pride, vanity, love of power.

Party platforms and presidential programs may win the chairman's support and when this occurs the President will sleep more soundly at night. As sometimes occurs, the chairman may be open-minded—or at least uncommitted on administration measures which fall within his committee's jurisdiction. In such instances, other things being equal, he may and usually will support or at least go along with the administration's wishes on the pragmatic ground that such co-operation will encourage reciprocal accommodation when the situation is reversed. In many instances, moreover, party loyalty will induce a committee chairman to support his chief even when he would prefer to do otherwise. Committee chairmen may or may not be dedicated party men, but if they have been re-elected enough times to move up the seniority ladder to the chairmanship post, they must be politicians with the instinct for survival. Frequently, this instinct works in favor of the President. When it does, he is fortunate. But whether it does or does not is often a factor beyond the President's control—a difficulty that he must always contemplate, a hazard that he cannot forestall or eradicate.[17]

Much has been written about congressional leadership, that is, the elected leadership of each chamber and the importance of fostering closer collaboration between that leadership and the President in achieving a more effective governmental mechanism. This is a valid objective but it is also a misleading description of the legislative process. Every President who has had strong legislative aspirations has been confronted with the task of establishing and maintaining satisfactory working relationships with the congressional leaders—more accurately the House and Senate leaders—because the problem is a dual one, requiring separate negotiations and separate treaties of alliance. Some Presidents have used one device, others another; some have succeeded in one chamber but failed in the other; some have been successful in certain periods or certain areas but unsuccessful in others. The patterns have been almost infinitely varied, depending upon ever changing factors of personality, circumstance, and luck. The important point for our purposes, however, is that regardless of the ups and downs of presidential-congressional collaboration at the leadership level, the standing committees have tended to function as a third force and they have not always been responsive to the top leadership and its collaborative enterprises. This has been equally true in both chambers.

David B. Truman's careful, discriminating study of congressional

---

[17] Some observers argue that the only real offenders are those committee chairmen who come from one-party states. These men have been able to impose narrow, unrepresentative views upon the enlightened majority of their fellow committee members, so the argument goes, thus defeating the true will of the people against the desires of an unhappy but helpless majority in the committee. This point of view has some validity; how much is difficult to say because no systematic study of standing committee chairmen has been made. Long terms of service in one-party states are common, and the seniority thus gained is reflected in the disproportionate number of standing committee chairmanships held by Southerners during periods of Democratic hegemony. On the other hand, such non-Southern figures as Borah, Lodge, McCarran, O'Connor, Taber, Taft, and Vandenberg—from both parties and both chambers—call to mind committee chairmen whose refusal to co-operate with presidential recommendations caused heartburn to the occupant of the White House.

behavior[18] has added much to our understanding of how Congress works, particularly about who are the influential figures in concerting action. His meticulous analysis reveals that the efforts of the elected leaders of each chamber to marshal party support on behalf of administration programs have met with some success. Their achievements have been singularly modest, however, and the most striking impression the findings convey is the absence of dependable guarantees. The centrifugal forces still appear to outweigh the unifying ones; the committees retain their power advantage, and the degree to which party programs can be achieved is problematical and uncertain. All the inducements available to the President plus the wide range of techniques of persuasion, direct and indirect, formal and informal, personal and political, exercised by the elective leaders fall well short of assuring success. It is no disparagement of the substantial improvement these concerted techniques have produced to acknowledge that at best presidential leadership in legislation still rests on shifting sands rather than on anything more substantial.

Is there any firm basis for believing that the principle of presidential leadership is gaining headway? That it is becoming more broadly based, more solidly embedded in our political mores? Is there evidence of cumulative growth—that the gains made by one President remain as a sedimentary deposit that hardens into a foundation stone on which succeeding Presidents can erect their own leadership structures? I think the answer is both yes and no. On the affirmative side one can point to the emerging recognition and qualified acceptance of the idea of presidential leadership in legislation even by Congress itself. Despite the protestations, exemplified by the declaration of Mr. Voorhis, Congress can never erase or ignore what has occurred during the past twenty-five years; history is never unmade, and the history of executive aggrandizement in legislation has left its residue. The steady growth of budget bureau activity in legislative clearance has strengthened executive, and correspondingly weakened congressional, bargaining power.

Congress cannot fully counteract budget bureau central clearance because it is incapable of presenting a competitive, unified view. Congress is limited by its protean, decentralized, fractionated approach to any problem. This weakens Congress' power to resist the President's unified program proposals because it cannot offer a full alternative program. But it is also a strength defensively because the President cannot meet and overcome Congress as a single opponent. He must deal with a host of recalcitrant barons, each with his own particular set of defensive resources. If the President had unlimited time and energy, he might vanquish each holdout one by one, but because he has so many other salients on which he must operate, he simply cannot prevail, so he must

[18] See n. 14.

settle for a few key victories and let the rest await another day. We thus come back to the problem of presidential-congressional relations, not as a problem of negotiated agreements between two or three top level plenipotentiaries, each with full powers, but rather as a multilateral process involving both kingly and ducal sovereignties.

These are the facts as they seem to operate. How do they come about? It is my contention that given the structural arrangements laid down in the Constitution, they are inevitable and inescapable. The President possesses no mechanical leverages adequate to overcome the structural forces making for independent action by the Congress. The federal factor, the separation of President and Congress, of House and Senate, the committee system, the link between each congressman and his constituency are structural barriers to presidential aspirations. Congressmen find reasons for opposing the President and they do not get penalized for doing so. Apparently, although they accept the idea of the President as leader, Americans do not accept his interference in making their electoral decisions concerning Congress. If the President *could* persuade voters to give him a *full mandate* by supporting only *his candidates* and defeating his enemies, our system *might* work as some desire despite its structural handicaps. In reality, however, it is fanciful to assume that—given existing structural arrangements, plus existing social, economic, demographic conditions—it will soon be possible for the President to receive this kind of full mandate from the electorate.[19] One may rail at voters for being irrational, inconsistent, illogical in their use of the ballot. Whether such strictures are true depends on one's point of view. There is no mathematical basis for deciding the issue. But

[19] Wilson recognized the centrifugal and disintegrating influences of standing committees and he advocated the legislative caucus as an effective countermeasure: "The caucus is meant as an antidote to the Committees. It is designed to supply the cohesive principle which the multiplicity and mutual independence of the Committees so powerfully tend to destroy. . . . The caucus is the drilling ground of the party. There its discipline is renewed and strengthened, its uniformity of step and gesture regained. The voting and speaking in the House are generally merely the movements of a sort of dress parade, for which the exercises of the caucus are designed to prepare. It is easy to see how difficult it would be for the party to keep its head amidst the cross-movements of the Committees without this now and again pulling itself together in caucus, where it can ask itself its own mind and pledge itself anew to eternal agreement" (*Congressional Government*, pp. 211–12). Ironically, Wilson, the President, was to learn that the formula laid down by Wilson, the political scientist, revealed serious operating deficiencies. For a very brief period, actually the first year of his administration, Wilson succeeded in invoking party discipline via the Democratic caucus in support of two major administration bills; thereafter his much-valued device was never invoked; the party unity that weighed so heavily in his thinking as an academic student of the American political system quickly proved to be a mirage when viewed in the harsh light of reality. Wilson reveals himself at his best and also at his worst in his extended discussion of party in the passage from which the preceding quotation is taken. The vigor, the mastery of figurative language, the elegant phrase, all combine to carry the reader along despite the fact that much of the substance not only is not true today, but was not true at the time it was written. One almost has the feeling that Wilson was the victim of his own eloquence.

assuming for the moment that the charge *may be true*, there is no *mechanism* (aside from the authoritarian device of a single list of candidates) for forcing the voter to behave logically.

The three Presidents during the twentieth century who have appealed most successfully to American voters as popular leaders are Wilson, Franklin D. Roosevelt, and Eisenhower. Each in his own way inspired confidence in his ability to cope with the baffling problems besetting the country. Yet each of these three men enjoyed the dubious distinction of being rebuffed by the electorate when, at the height of his popularity, he attempted to influence the selection of members of Congress. The years 1918, 1938, and 1958 stand out as conspicuous tombstones marking the disastrous ventures in winning a presidential mandate by creating a presidential party.

Some will argue—Burns and others have—that there has never been a careful, systematic, sustained attempt to organize a presidential party and that until such an effort has been made no one can say with certainty that it cannot be done. This is the central thesis of the constructive portion of *Roosevelt: The Lion and the Fox*—that President Roosevelt did not avail himself of the rich opportunity he had in 1936 and after. It is idle now to speculate on what might have occurred had Roosevelt followed the line Burns and others urged. The fact that Mr. Roosevelt did not choose to make such an attempt is not without significance. He had already shown that he was not bound by tradition and he certainly did not have any deep-seated reverence for or loyalty to the Democratic party. One cannot but wonder whether from where he sat and viewed the national political scene—against the background of political sociology which he understood so well—he concluded that any attempt to construct a presidential party would not be worth the effort.

III

I have argued that structural features of our government have produced certain operating characteristics. Before concluding, however, I wish to consider very briefly the underlying question: Are our structural characteristics necessarily structural inadequacies? In other words, have they served us poorly or well?

The problems and obstacles which seem to embarrass the President in his efforts to employ the power of the United States in the interests of its people are real in the sense that they actually do exist, but their sociological significance is not always kept in mind. Within our Congress are reflected the multitude of interests that go to make up this large, variegated, complex country. They are the components of a free society—the factions about which Madison wrote in the *Federalist*, No. 10. They are the concomitants of our social system, not of our particular governmental forms. This is the essential fact, yet it is frequently over-looked or ignored in the critiques of our governmental structure. As a human agency for meeting social demands, government must face the structural problem of providing a mechanism that permits and promotes the full expression of these social demands and translates them into public policy. The important question, therefore, is whether, given the sociological preconditions, our particular governmental arrangements—our structural mechanisms—are adequate or faulty.

I would have to argue that even though our legislative-executive insti-tutional arrangement as conceived by the framers was intended primari-ly to function as a restraint upon legislation rather than as a facilitation and even though the machinery has evolved in ways uncontemplated by its creators, the mechanism wrought by them has been satisfactory. Through it many segments of our pluralistic society have expressed their varied needs; through it competition and conflict have produced negotiation and accommodation; through it an impressive amount of constructive public policy has been achieved; through it changed con-ditions have been adjusted to.

None of these things has been done perfectly; no single piece of legislation has pleased everybody, indeed very few laws have *fully* pleased anybody. This is not ideal; it is not really satisfying, but I think it *is* satisfactory. Tocqueville's comment is wholly apposite and truly profound: "The early stages of national existence are the only periods at which it is possible to make legislation strictly logical; and when we perceive a nation in the enjoyment of this advantage, we should not hastily conclude that it is wise, but only remember that it is young."[20]

It seems doubtful that any other governmental mechanism would have performed its functions better than those we have. This does not mean that our system is perfect or that our congressmen are philosopher kings. As a group they have probably discharged their responsibilities as well as any group of human beings can reasonably be expected to do, and the institutional arrangements provided in the Constitution, far from being obstacles, have contributed constructively to the viability of our political system.

[20] Tocqueville, *op. cit.*, I, 119.

ALPHEUS THOMAS MASON

Myth and Reality in Supreme Court Decisions

T HE SUPREME COURT's decision of March 26, 1962, in the historic
case of *Baker* v. *Carr*[1] is a notable step in making rotten boroughs subject
to judicial correction. For the first time the Court held that voters,
whose franchise is diluted by unfair, unequal, or discriminatory appor-
tionment of legislative seats, may seek relief in the federal courts. Enforcement of constitutional limitations in an area heretofore free from
judicial intervention stimulated a significant colloquy between Justices
Frankfurter, now retired, and Clark as to how the Court can best
maintain popular confidence and respect. Frankfurter deplored "as a
massive repudiation of the experience of our whole past," the Court's
belated assumption of responsibility for a more equitable system of
representation. Judicial invasion of this "political thicket" would, he
suggested, "impair the Court's position as the ultimate organ of 'the
supreme Law of the Land.' "[2] Describing Frankfurter's dissent as
"bursting with words that go through so much and conclude with so
little,"[3] Clark observed: "I would not consider intervention by this
Court into so delicate a field if there were any other relief available to
the people of Tennessee. But the majority of the people of Tennessee
have no practical opportunities for exerting their political weight at the
polls."[4] Frankfurter's solution was an "informed, civically militant electorate" and "an aroused popular conscience."[5] But, Clark countered,
these long continued electoral injustices do not, in fact, "sear 'the conscience of the people's representatives.' "[6] Reverting to Frankfurter's
cherished principle of judicial self-restraint, Clark concluded: "It is well

ALPHEUS THOMAS MASON is McCormick Professor of Jurisprudence at Princeton
University.

Reprinted from *Virginia Law Review*, XLVIII, No. 8 (December, 1962), 1385–1406.

[1] 369 U.S. 186 (1962).

[2] *Id.* at 267 (dissenting opinion).

[3] *Id.* at 251 (concurring opinion).

[4] *Id.* at 258–59 (concurring opinion).

[5] *Id.* at 270 (dissenting opinion).

[6] *Id.* at 259 (concurring opinion).

for this Court to practice self-restraint and discipline in constitutional adjudication, but never in its history have those principles received sanction where the national rights of so many have been so clearly infringed for so long a time. National respect for the courts is more enhanced through the forthright enforcement of those rights [equitable representation] rather than by rendering them nugatory through the interposition of subterfuges."[7]

With the triumph of Justice Clark's realistic approach, the American ideal of political equality came closer to realization. By enforcing the constitutional limitations in the Fourteenth Amendment's equal protection clause, the Court functioned as an instrument of democracy and of majority rule. This dramatic struggle between myth and reality represents a familiar contest in the annals of the judiciary.

Man lives by symbols.[8] Bewildered by political imponderables, he requires firm emotional support. The contribution of government depends in part on its form. "Royalty," Walter Bagehot has written, "is a government in which the attention of the nation is concentrated on one person doing interesting actions. A Republic is a government in which that attention is divided between many, who are all doing uninteresting actions."[9] Americans find in the Supreme Court a sense of security not unlike that instilled by the British crown. Nine black-robed Justices conjure up the image of equal justice under law, saving us from both the tyranny of the multitude and the arrogance of personal government.

Monarchy strengthens government "with the strength of religion."[10] By making the Constitution seem like a vehicle of inspired revelation, the Court performs a similar service in America. Excepting the Constitution itself, the Supreme Court is "the country's greatest symbol of orderly, stable and righteous government."[11] Like a queen on the throne, it stirs interest and imagination, and creates in the citizen profound respect and confidence. But there is a difference, and an important one: the British monarch does not govern. Parliament and the cabinet are the working parts of the political system. In England distinct roles are played by different institutions. In the United States these functions are blended. The Court is both symbol and instrument of authority. The American counterpart of the British crown has real power; the Supreme Court can bring Congress, President, state governors and legislators to heel.

[7] *Id.* at 262 (concurring opinion).

[8] HOLMES, *John Marshall*, in COLLECTED LEGAL PAPERS 270 (1920).

[9] BAGEHOT, THE ENGLISH CONSTITUTION AND OTHER POLITICAL ESSAYS 107 (rev. ed. 1872).

[10] *Ibid.*

[11] *Hearings on S. 1392 before the Senate Committee on the Judiciary*, 75th Cong., 1st Sess. 233 (1937).

Mingling the occult and power aspects of governing in a single instrument leads to confusion. The Court has been called the most revered and the least understood of all our political institutions. In our tripartite constitutional system, the Supreme Court is the Holy of Holies. In the public eye, Supreme Court Justices are "brushed with divinity."[12] "I reckon him one of the worst enemies of the community," Charles Evans Hughes once remarked, "who will talk lightly of the dignity of the bench."[13] Public confidence in the Court and popular respect for its decisions can best be maintained by a reverential stance. One recalls Edmund Burke's caveat as to the proper attitude toward the British constitution: "We ought to understand it according to our measure, and to venerate where we are not able presently to comprehend."[14]

The Court as a revered symbol stems in part from the effort to resolve what the late Robert H. Jackson once described as a "basic inconsistency between popular government and judicial supremacy."[15] The Founding Fathers subscribed to the proposition that just governments derive their powers from the consent of the governed. At the same time, they apparently sanctioned Charles Evans Hughes's much quoted dictum that "the Constitution is what the judges say it is."[16] The republican principle does not require an "unqualified complaisance to every sudden breeze of passion."[17] Various constitutional devices, including judicial review, enthrone a "deliberate sense of the community," not "transient impulse," as the standard governing those intrusted with the management of public affairs.[18] In the achievement of this objective, the Court plays an important part. Having won final authority, against the claims of the President or Congress, to say what the Constitution means, it justifies this power by the fiction that the Court is merely requiring other agencies of government to subordinate themselves to a self-evident Constitution which, in some miraculous way, coincides, at the particular moment of decision, with the judicial version of it. Judicial review thus becomes American democracy's way of covering its bet.[19]

To render more palatable this oligarchic element in our politics, the Court evolved the theory that judges exercise only judgment, not will.

[12] FRANK, COURTS ON TRIAL 255 (1949).

[13] Address by Charles Evans Hughes before the Elmira Chamber of Commerce, May 3, 1907, in ADDRESSES AND PAPERS OF CHARLES EVANS HUGHES 33, 139 (1908).

[14] BURKE, *An Appeal from the New to the Old Whigs*, in IV THE WRITINGS AND SPEECHES OF EDMUND BURKE 57, 213 (1908).

[15] Jackson, *Preface* to JACKSON, THE STRUGGLE FOR JUDICIAL SUPREMACY, at vii (1941).

[16] HUGHES, *op. cit. supra* note 13, at 139.

[17] THE FEDERALIST No. 71, at 446 (Lodge ed. 1888) (Hamilton).

[18] *Ibid.*

[19] Corwin, 56 HARV. L. REV. 484, 487 (1942).

"Judicial power," Chief Justice Marshall declared, "is never exercised for the purpose of giving effect to the will of the Judge; always for the purpose of giving effect to the will of the . . . law."[20] "The thrill is irresistible," Judge Cardozo remarked on this passage; "we feel the mystery and the awe of inspired revelation."[21] So the myth was born and consecrated. It has been exploded again and again by the Court's own action, and yet it survives.

Americans assume that it is possible to achieve through courts an ideal of British origin: James Harrington's vaunted "empire of laws and not of men." Sir Edward Coke conceded that God had endowed His Majesty with "excellent science, and great endowments of nature," but the king "was not learned in the laws of his realm," a unique endowment of artificial reason and judgment, requiring long study and experience.[22] Alexander Hamilton noted that judicial competence entailed such "long and laborious study" that few men would qualify for "the stations of judges."[23] To legislators and executives, the Constitution's dictates are hidden and obscure. Its only authoritative mouthpiece is the United States Supreme Court. Every judicial version of the supreme law, gleaned from a sort of brooding omnipresence, has the special virtue of never mangling or changing the original instrument.

Such legerdemain, still a recognized tenet in our legal lore,[24] poses a well-nigh insuperable task. Judicial decisions must be recognized as synonymous with constitutional imperatives. When the Justices handed down their explosive decision of 1793,[25] taking jurisdiction of a case in which a South Carolina citizen sued the sovereign state of Georgia, there could be only one solution—amend the Constitution. The ruling ran counter to the desires of the people and to the expressed intentions of the framers;[26] but it was believed that the document of 1789, not its interpretation by judges, was at fault. A few years later, however, the Justices themselves acknowledged fallibility. In *Calder* v. *Bull*[27] Justices Chase and Iredell emphasized that the Court would declare no acts unconstitutional except in a very clear case, a warning to succeeding judges to keep their power within bounds lest judicial magic be undermined by their own hands. The task proved to be beyond their powers.

[20] Osborn v. Bank of the United States, 22 U.S. (9 Wheat.) 738, 866 (1824).

[21] CARDOZO, LAW AND LITERATURE AND OTHER ESSAYS AND ADDRESSES 11 (1931).

[22] Prohibitions del Roy, xii Coke 63, 77 Eng. Rep. 1342 (1608).

[23] THE FEDERALIST No. 78, at 496 (Wright ed. 1961).

[24] See Arthur Miller's iconoclastic, *A Note on the Supreme Court Decisions*, 10 J. PUB. L. 139–51 (1961).

[25] Chisholm v. Georgia, 2 U.S. (2 Dall.) 419 (1793).

[26] See Hans v. Louisiana, 134 U.S. 1, 12–14 (1890).

[27] 3 U.S. (3 Dall.) 386 (1798).

In his book of 1928 on the Supreme Court, Charles Evans Hughes singled out three cases—Dred Scott, Legal Tender, and Pollock—in which the Court signally failed to achieve this coincidence and, as a consequence, "suffered severely from self-inflicted wounds."[28] The Dred Scott[29] ruling of 1857 caused injury by making the Supreme Court seem like a citadel of slavocracy. The Legal Tender[30] decision of 1870 was damaging because it overturned a precedent of only two years' standing by only one vote and as a direct result of the appointment of two new judges after the first decision came down. The third wound was perhaps the most serious, for a single judge's change of mind after reargument resulted in voiding the federal income tax by a vote of five to four.[31] Deploring this myth-shattering record, Hughes commented: "Stability in judicial opinions is of no little importance in maintaining respect for the Court's work."[32]

The remedies resorted to for correcting these judicial wrongs put further strain on magic. When the Court declared in 1857 that Negro slavery was immune to destruction by Congress, the people were obliged to wipe that judgment from the record by resort to the sword and the arduous process of constitutional amendment. When the Court told them in the Legal Tender case of 1870 that the means Congress had devised for saving the country from bankruptcy and financial ruin was invalid, the President merely appointed new judges of a different persuasion and obtained an acceptable result. By a vote of five to four in the Income Tax cases of 1895, the national government lost a source of revenue every country on earth possesses. The people accepted it. Equating the decision with the Constitution, they turned with Job-like patience to the task of escaping this arbitrary judgment by the tedious process of formal amendment. After Congress had exhausted its resources in the vain effort to end child labor, the people waited nearly a generation before learning that the Tenth Amendment, interposed as a constitutional block in 1918[33] and again in 1922,[34] was merely a "truism."[35] Meanwhile, repeated efforts had been made to amend the Constitution, permitting Congress to banish the scourge. In 1941 it was discovered

[28] Hughes, The Supreme Court of the United States: Its Foundations, Methods and Achievements 50 (1928).

[29] Scott v. Sandford, 60 U.S. (19 How.) 393 (1857).

[30] Knox v. Lee, 79 U.S. (12 Wall.) 457 (1870).

[31] Pollock v. Farmers' Loan & Trust Co., 158 U.S. 601, *reversing on rehearing*, 157 U.S. 429 (1895).

[32] Hughes, *op. cit. supra* note 28, at 53.

[33] Hammer v. Dagenhart, 247 U.S. 251 (1918).

[34] Bailey v. Drexel Furniture Co., 259 U.S. 20 (1922).

[35] United States v. Darby, 312 U.S. 100, 124 (1941).

that a power the Court had earlier found wanting had existed all the while.[36] These are but a few occasions when the people have remained calm under circumstances that threatened to make the idea of self-government a mockery. The people not only exercised remarkable self-restraint but through all of these frustrations they remained firmly attached to the Court as the symbol of justice. But there have been moments of doubt.

The Court as the Constitution's unimpeachable mouthpiece met the first real test in the political upsurge which took shape as the Jacksonian revolution. Querying the federalist theory that the people's will, embodied in the Constitution, is discoverable only by judges, Jacksonians stressed the idea of popular sovereignty asserted at the ballot box and in legislative halls. The police power, a broad authority in the state legislatures "to govern men and things," emerged as a juristic expression of popular sovereignty. Threatened were solid American values summed up under the rubric "vested rights"—the notion voiced by judges that they would disallow any legislative act encroaching with undue harshness on existing property rights.[37] Enmeshed in the very warp and woof of American constitutionalism, this doctrine was hard to reconcile with the state police power. What happens when an irresistible movement —popular sovereignty and the police power—encounters an immovable object—vested rights? Faced with this impasse, the Justices had two alternatives: they could discard the vested rights doctrine, as limiting legislative power, or cast about for a restrictive formula within the written Constitution itself, and thus retain supervisory control.

By the mid-nineteenth century "due process," a conveniently vague concept found in many state constitutions, was sometimes resorted to as a constitutional barrier capable of damming the rising tide of Jacksonian democracy. There were, it was said, certain "absolute private rights," including those of property, beyond the reach of popular majorities.[38] A legislature may exceed its powers, even though it complies with the forms and procedures which belong to "due process."[39] Flouted was the generally accepted notion that "due process" connotes only procedural limitations. In time it was interpreted as setting limits on what *can* be done as well as on *how* something must be done. This judicial transformation stirred vehement objection. To invoke this clause

[36] United States v. Darby, 312 U.S. 100 (1941).

[37] See CORWIN, THE TWILIGHT OF THE SUPREME COURT 52-101 (1934). For a valuable study of the conflict between public power and private rights in the late nineteenth century, see PAUL, CONSERVATIVE CRISIS AND THE RULE OF LAW: ATTITUDES OF BAR AND BENCH, 1887–1895 (1960).

[38] Wynehamer v. The People, 13 N.Y. 378, 387 (1856).

[39] See *id.* at 420.

as a substantive bar would result, it was argued, in decisions based solely on judicial discretion.[40]

Until the adoption of the Fourteenth Amendment in 1868, the Constitution contained no "due process" clause restricting state power. In early cases arising under this provision, the Supreme Court maintained a hands-off position, refusing to act as censor of regulatory state legislation. If a statute passed muster in terms of procedural requirements, aggrieved litigants were told that their remedy against abuses was "resort to the polls, not to the courts."[41]

Dissenting judges protested loudly. The issue of public power versus property rights seemed to them crucial. In 1878 the American Bar Association was organized, and promptly embarked on a campaign of education designed to reverse the Court's broad conception of legislative power and, correspondingly, to expand the role of courts. Lawyers and judges were determined to recapture what the Jacksonian revolution had partially repudiated—their special responsibility for construing the Constitution. Addressing the Bar Association's second annual meeting, President Edward J. Phelps deplored the increasing number of instances in which unhallowed hands had been placed upon that sacred document. The Constitution, he said, had become

more and more a subject to be hawked about the country, debated in the newspapers, discussed from the stump, elucidated by pot house politicians, and dunghill editors, scholars in the science of government who have never found leisure for the graces of English grammar or the embellishments of correct spelling.[42]

Exclusive interpretation of the Constitution must be regained for that "inner sanctum," that "priestly tribe"—the American Bar.

The campaign succeeded. Beginning about 1890, Supreme Court Justices became high-level politicians. Exercising under the broad clauses of the Constitution, especially "due process," a supervisory role over public policy, they annexed the functions of a "super-legislature." At the same time they continued the pretense of doing no more than applying the clear command of the Constitution, provoking the late Thomas Reed Powell's wry comment, "that these judicial professions of automatism are most insistent when it is most obvious that they are being honored in the breach rather than in the observance."[43] Coinciding with

[40] *Id.* at 432 (dissenting opinion).

[41] Munn v. Illinois, 94 U.S. 113, 134 (1877).

[42] Speech by Edward J. Phelps, American Bar Association Annual Meeting, August 1879, in 2 A.B.A. REP. 173, 190 (1879). See, in this connection, Corwin, *The Debt of American Constitutional Law to Natural Law Concepts*, 25 NOTRE DAME LAW. 258, 258–84, 278–79 (1950) and TWISS, LAWYERS AND THE CONSTITUTION (1950).

[43] POWELL, VAGARIES AND VARIETIES IN CONSTITUTIONAL INTERPRETATION 43 (1956).

judicial aggrandizement was a marked rise in the use of robes.[44] About the same time, too, the original Constitution, heretofore "kept folded up in a little tin box in the lower part of a closet" in the State Department, was placed on public view.[45] These coincidences are the more remarkable in light of the fact that what was being enforced was not the Constitution but the laissez faire dogma of Herbert Spencer and William Graham Sumner. Strict observance of laissez faire meant progress; violation of it spelled disaster. Natural law—the inevitability of the human struggle, the survival of the fittest in the economic no less than in the biological world—replaced the Constitution.

Justice David J. Brewer cited "the black flag of anarchism, flaunting destruction to property," and "the red flag of socialism, inviting a redistribution of property."[46] Noting that the friends of "mere numbers" were "unanimous in crying out against judicial interference, and are constantly seeking to minimize the power of the courts," Brewer raised the question "whether, in view of this exigency, the functions of the judiciary should be strengthened and enlarged, or weakened and restricted."[47] His answer was unequivocal—"strengthen the judiciary."[48] No untoward consequences could be expected to follow from the Court's assumption of a policy-determining function, Brewer suggested, since the people are unaware that the Court possesses it. Nevertheless great care had to be taken lest Court decisions affecting controversial public issues be seen as the result of judicial fiat, not of constitutional commands.

It was suggested, for example, that the income tax decision might be reversed by a mere act of Congress. Discussion of this proposal reached its height during the presidency of William Howard Taft. Senator Joseph Bailey of Texas introduced a corrective measure as an amendment to the tariff bill. Said Senator Bailey:

[I]nstead of trying to conform the amendment to the decision of the court, the amendment distinctly challenges that decision. I do not believe that that opinion is a correct interpretation of the Constitution. . . . With this thought in my mind, and remembering that the decision was by a bare majority, and that the decision itself overruled the decisions of a hundred years . . . I think that the

[44] See Frank, *The Cult of the Robe*, Saturday Rev., Oct. 13, 1945, p. 13; also in FRANK, COURTS ON TRIAL 254 (1949).

[45] JAMESON, AN INTRODUCTION TO THE STUDY OF THE CONSTITUTIONAL AND POLITICAL HISTORY OF THE STATES 5 (Johns Hopkins University Studies in Historical and Political Science Ser. 4, No. 5, 1886).

[46] Address by Judge David J. Brewer, New York State Bar Association Annual Meeting, Jan. 17, 1893, in XVI PROCEEDINGS OF THE NEW YORK STATE BAR ASSOCIATION 37, 47 (1893).

[47] *Id.* at 42.

[48] *Id.* at 44.

court, upon a reconsideration of this question, will adjudge an income tax a constitutional exercise of power by Congress.[49]

The President himself considered the Court's decision erroneous, but advised against this easy escape. "Although I have not considered a constitutional amendment as necessary to the exercise of certain phases of this power," Taft explained,

a mature consideration has satisfied me that an amendment is the only proper course for its establishment to its full extent. . . . This course is much to be preferred to the one proposed of re-enacting a law once judicially declared to be unconstitutional. For the Congress to assume that the court will reverse itself, and to enact legislation on such an assumption, will not strengthen popular confidence in the stability of judicial construction of the Constitution. It is much wiser policy to accept the decision and remedy the defect by amendment in due and regular course.[50]

Senator Root of New York, agreeing with the President, pointed out the damage that would result from congressional reversal. A by-product would be

a campaign of oratory upon the stump, of editorials in the press, of denunciation and imputation designed to compel that great tribunal to yield to the force of the opinion of the executive and the legislative branches. . . . If they refuse to yield, what then? A breach between the two parts of our Government, with popular acclaim behind the popular branch, all setting against the independence, the dignity, the respect, the sacredness of that great tribunal whose function in our system of government has made us unlike any republic that ever existed in the world. . . .[51]

The fiction of an unchanging Constitution, save by the formal process of amendment, had to be preserved even in the face of a judicial decision that did incalculable damage to it. Neither President Taft nor Senator Root was under the illusion that the law either is or can be stationary and certain, but both were wary of encouraging the notion that Congress alone could reverse an objectionable decision. "It is one of the essential weaknesses of the Government by Judiciary," Louis B. Boudin comments with callous irreverence,

that, as in all theocratic governments, based upon the sole power to expound a sacred text, its priests cannot afford to admit error without undermining the power of the priesthood and upsetting the form of government in which they are the ruling caste. Error must therefore be perpetuated, no matter what the consequences.[52]

[49] 44 Cong. Rec. 1351 (1909). See *id.* at 4394 (remarks of Representative Pickett); *id.* at 4396 (remarks of Representative James); *id.* at 4401 (remarks of Representative Hull).

[50] S. Doc. No. 98, 61st Cong., 1st Sess. 2 (1909).

[51] 44 Cong. Rec. 4003 (1909) (remarks of Senator Root).

[52] 2 Boudin, Government by Judiciary 287–88 (1932).

The United States Senate acknowledged the fiction of judicial impotence and co-operated in keeping it alive. When Woodrow Wilson appointed Louis D. Brandeis to the high bench in 1916, the opposition quickly formed ranks in an attempt to prevent confirmation.[53] Of course the real danger was Brandeis' presumably radical social and economic convictions. Yet the battle could not be fought on this ground. That would have portrayed the Court as a third chamber of the legislature. But if the Justices' professions of helplessness be true, why should there have been such an uproar against Brandeis? If courts, in deciding the cases coming before them, exert no more discretion than the dry-goods salesman measuring out calico or the grocer weighing coffee, why should the appointee's social and economic views be relevant? Neither Brandeis' supporters nor his opponents were prepared to admit that social philosophy and economic predilection are crucial in the work of a Supreme Court Justice. Both were under the spell of the judicial refrain —judges are mere instruments of the law and can will nothing.

By 1920, this fiction was beginning to show signs of wear. In 1905, Justice Holmes had charged that the majority's preferences obtruded into judicial decisions.[54] Others began to fear judicial bias of a different brand. Aware that the winner of the 1920 presidential election would have an opportunity to reconstitute the Supreme Court, and much disturbed by Bull Moose and other forms of "progressivism," William Howard Taft opened the door to the sanctum sanctorum. In a campaign speech, he remarked: "There is no greater domestic issue in this election than the maintenance of the Supreme Court as the bulwark to enforce the guaranty that no man shall be deprived of his property without due process of law."[55]

Warren G. Harding won the presidency by an electoral landslide. The next year Taft himself moved into the center chair on the high bench and began immediately to use his influence to secure the appointment of colleagues whose views were in accord with his own. Judges Benjamin N. Cardozo and Learned Hand were among the names mentioned for vacancies, but the Chief Justice, fearing that they might "herd" with Holmes and Brandeis, voiced his objections.[56] "The Constitution was intended . . . ," the Chief Justice declared, "to prevent experimentation with the fundamental rights of the individual."[57] Sym-

---

[53] See MASON, BRANDEIS: A FREE MAN'S LIFE 465–508 (1946), for a detailed account of the controversy that arose when Brandeis was appointed to the Supreme Court.

[54] Lochner v. New York, 198 U.S. 45, 74 (1905) (dissenting opinion).

[55] Taft, *Mr. Wilson and the Campaign*, 10 YALE REV. 1, 19–20 (1920).

[56] See Murphy, *In His Own Image: Mr. Chief Justice Taft and Supreme Court Appointments*, 1961 SUPREME COURT REV. 159, 178–79.

[57] Truax v. Corrigan, 257 U.S. 312, 338 (1921).

bolism would help Supreme Court Justices to enforce this theory. "It is well," Taft observed,

that judges should be clothed in robes, not only, that those who witness the administration of justice should be properly advised that the function performed is one different from, and higher, than that which a man discharges as a citizen in the ordinary walks of life; but also, in order to impress the judge himself with the constant consciousness that he is a high-priest in the temple of justice and is surrounded with obligations of a sacred character that he cannot escape and that require his utmost care, attention and self-suppression.[58]

But judicial robes did not hide from a growing number of insurgent lawmakers the power-crippling nature of judicial authority.

Senator George W. Norris lifted the veil in 1925, opposing confirmation of Harlan Fiske Stone as Associate Justice because J. P. Morgan and Company had once been Stone's client. In the 1924 presidential election the American people had indicated their preference for a Vermont farmer rather than a Morgan lawyer. "They did not know then ...," the Nebraska senator argued, "that instead of putting in the White House for four years an Executive who represented the Morgan interests, their action meant putting on the Supreme Bench for life another attorney of Morgan & Co."[59] Now the shoe was on the other foot.

The insurgents continued the drive with renewed vigor in 1930, fiercely protesting the confirmation of Charles Evans Hughes as Chief Justice. Casting aside the restraint that marked the debates on Brandeis, Senator Dill of Washington observed prophetically: "If the system of judicial law that is being written in defiance of State legislation and of congressional legislation is continued ... there is no human power in America that can keep the Supreme Court from becoming a political issue, nation-wide, in the not far-distant future."[60] Judicial theology was no longer sacrosanct. By calling attention to the discretionary power of Supreme Court Justices, the lawmakers hoped to destroy "the hush-hush and ah-ah atmosphere" shielding that political and very human institution. In protesting Hughes's confirmation, they tried "to strip away the absurd notion that judges are invested with a sanctity that puts them above ... criticism."[61]

"There has not been a criticism of the Supreme Court anywhere, even on the floor of the Senate, for several years ...," Norris explained,

because we have set it up on a pedestal beyond human criticism. ... We have made idols of the [Justices]. ... [T]hey have black gowns over their persons. Then they become something more than human beings. ...

[58] TAFT, PRESENT DAY PROBLEMS 63–64 (1908).

[59] 66 CONG. REC. 3053 (1925).

[60] 72 CONG. REC. 3642 (1930). [61] LIEF, DEMOCRACY'S NORRIS 347 (1939).

. . . [W]e have tried to make plain that the power of the Supreme Court . . . has been gradually growing: that, like human beings, they have been reaching out for more and more power until it has become common knowledge that they legislate and that they fix policies.[62]

Even professors of constitutional law now recognized that judges are engaged in the business of lawmaking, even Constitution-making. In his 1930 edition of *The Constitution and What It Means Today*, Professor Edward S. Corwin asserted: "[J]udicial review, far from being an instrument for the application of the Constitution, tends to supplant it. *In other words, the discretion of the Judges tends to supplant it.*"[63] That same year, Professor Frankfurter of the Harvard Law School declared that "the Supreme Court *is* the Constitution."[64] "[L]et us face the fact," Frankfurter commented bluntly, "that five Justices of the Supreme Court *are* molders of policy, rather than impersonal vehicles of revealed truth."[65]

Meanwhile the Justices themselves were impugning judicial objectivity. In 1924, Justice Brandeis complained that the Court, transcending the "function of judicial review," had annexed "powers of a super-legislature."[66] In 1930, Justice Holmes declared that he could see hardly any limit but the "sky" to the elimination of legislation which struck "a majority of this Court as for any reason undesirable."[67] In May, 1936, when five Justices nullified a law so humane that few would dare oppose it, the minority exploded. For the Court's decision setting aside the New York minimum wage law for women, the dissenters found it difficult to imagine grounds "other than our own economic predilections. . . ."[68] Dissenting Justices then drove home the very point raucous senators had stressed in 1925 and 1930. They avowed that "the only check upon our own exercise of power is our own sense of self-restraint."[69]

While Stone and other dissenting Justices told tales out of school, certain of their colleagues continued the conventional pose. In 1936, Justice Roberts told the nation's farmers that all the Court had to do in passing on the validity of the Agricultural Adjustment Act was to "lay

[62] 72 Cong. Rec. 3645 (1930).

[63] Corwin, *Preface* to Corwin, The Constitution and What It Means Today (4th ed. 1930).

[64] Frankfurter, *The United States Supreme Court Molding the Constitution*, 32 Current History 235, 240 (1930).

[65] Frankfurter, *The Supreme Court and The Public*, 83 Forum 329, 334 (1930).

[66] Jay Burns Baking Co. v. Bryan, 264 U.S. 504, 534 (1924) (dissenting opinion).

[67] Baldwin v. Missouri, 281 U.S. 586, 595 (1930) (dissenting opinion).

[68] Morehead v. New York *ex rel.* Tipaldo, 298 U.S. 587, 633 (1936) (Stone, J., dissenting).

[69] United States v. Butler, 297 U.S. 1, 79 (1936) (Stone, J., dissenting).

the article of the Constitution which is invoked beside the statute which is challenged and to decide whether the latter squares with the former." The only power the Court has, "if such it may be called, is the power of judgment."[70] Justice Sutherland denounced Stone's disclosures as "both ill considered and mischievous." "Self-restraint," Sutherland insisted, "belongs in the domain of will and not of judgment."[71] When the Court upsets "desirable" legislation, the blame rests squarely on the Constitution of 1789, not upon the Justices who chance to be its interpreters.[72] Sutherland's caveat recalls Cardozo's somewhat disdainful comment of 1931:

Judges march at times to pitiless conclusions under the prod of a remorseless logic which is supposed to leave them no alternative. They deplore the sacrificial rite. They perform it, none the less, with averted gaze, convinced as they plunge the knife that they obey the bidding of their office. The victim is offered up to the gods of jurisprudence on the altar of regularity.[73]

Stone had been guilty of an unforgivable sin. His suggestion that judges could and should restrain themselves dispelled the aura of sanctity, revealing behind judicial pageantry nine human beings, all participants in the governing process and no nearer the source of ultimate wisdom than others. The great vice of Stone's loose talk lay in its elimination of the hard and fast distinction between judgment and will. Public confidence was thereby jeopardized. For, once the mystery that surrounds judicial doings is penetrated, once the public recognizes the personal nature of judicial power, it might become difficult for the judiciary to function at all. One recalls Hans Christian Andersen's fable of the royal robes which could be seen only by the loyal, the pure, and the righteous. Justice Stone was the urchin who blurted out the facts.

Judicial decisions setting aside legislation which the Constitution did not forbid revealed how the symbol of the many had become "the instrument of the few."[74] Political decisions encouraged a political remedy. Forgetting Flaubert's subtle warning, "Il ne faut pas toucher aux idoles; la dorure en reste aux mains," President Roosevelt launched his ill-fated "court-packing" proposal. Stunned by this unholy blast, a great host rallied in protest. Over a period of five months Americans witnessed one of the most confused and confusing political controversies in our history. Everyone who could read knew that the nine Justices

---

[70] *Id.* at 63.

[71] West Coast Hotel Co. v. Parrish, 300 U.S. 379, 402 (1937) (dissenting opinion).

[72] *Id.* at 404 (dissenting opinion).

[73] CARDOZO, THE GROWTH OF THE LAW 66 (1924).

[74] Corwin, *The Constitution as Instrument and as Symbol*, 30 AM. POL. SCI. REV. 1071, 1080 (1936).

were not the nine vestal virgins of the Constitution. Through the years evidence mounted proving that judges, not fundamental law, shackled the power to govern. Yet the people had superstitiously come to regard the Court as the emblem of freedom and security. Tarnished though the symbol was, it, like the English monarchy, made for national stability, for poise and balance in crisis. Like its English counterpart, the Court commanded dogged loyalty of the citizenry. Overnight Supreme Court Justices were once more seen as demigods far above the sweaty crowd, abstractly weighing public issues in the delicate scales of law. The near-deathblow to the mythology came when, under the lash of an impulsive chief executive, the Court backtracked, surrendered, switched in time— Thomas Reed Powell put it—to save nine. Both before and after the assault, the high priests themselves helped to pull down the temple.

In their desperate attempt to destroy the New Deal, five, sometimes six, Justices had thrust themselves into the vortex of political controversy, exposing what they had sought so anxiously to disguise—that judicial decisions are, in fact, born out of the travail of economic and political conflict. The nation interpreted the judicial reversals of 1937 as approximating revolution. Yet Chief Justice Hughes insisted that the Court had not veered an inch from the course charted by the Constitution. "Stability in judicial opinions," so important in "maintaining respect for the Court's work," had not been jeopardized at all. Commentators were incredulous. Hughes's famous aphorism of 1907—"We are under a Constitution, but the Constitution is what the Judges say it is . . ."[75]—was widely quoted. The Chief Justice's decisions were cited as the perfect context to prove it. In bitter protest, he complained, as his biographer put it, that the critics were exposing "the solemn function of judging as a sort of humbuggery."[76] Hughes performed the seemingly impossible task of keeping the myth intact while shattering it almost beyond repair. As a magician, the Chief Justice was quicker than the eye.[77]

The mystery of the judicial process had once again been penetrated. It was now increasingly evident that the Supreme Court operated within the ambit of political considerations. Reaffirmed was Felix Frankfurter's realistic analysis before donning the robes: "[C]onstitutional law . . . is not at all a science, but applied politics. . . ."[78]

Though the Court's political role was revealed, its symbolic status

[75] Address by Charles Evans Hughes before the Elmira Chamber of Commerce, May 3, 1907, in Addresses and Papers of Charles Evans Hughes 133, 139 (1908).

[76] 1 Pusey, Charles Evans Hughes 204 (1951).

[77] See Mason, The Supreme Court from Taft to Warren 109–10 (1958).

[78] Law and Politics—Occasional Papers of Felix Frankfurter 6 (MacLeish and Prichard eds. 1939). John Chipman Gray, who is better known for his rigid rules of real property law, once characterized constitutional law as being "not law at all but politics." Dumbauld, *Judicial Review and Popular Sovereignty*, 99 U. Pa. L. Rev. 197, 208 (1950).

was not totally destroyed. The traditional reverence remains. A critic may lash out at particular decisions and still venerate the Court as an institution. Virginia congressman Burr P. Harrison, signer of the March, 1956, Southern Manifesto, criticized the desegregation decision of 1954 but objected to the proposal that the Chief Justice of the United States should report from time to time on "the state of the federal judiciary." The effect would be to "inject our Judges into politics." "[A]n air of detachment," the congressman insisted, "is precisely what is to be prized in the men who run our courts. Let us leave our Chief Justice on the cool heights of Olympus. . . ."[79] As a law teacher, Professor Frankfurter discussed the Court's political role realistically. On the bench, however, he voiced concern lest judicial sanctity be dispelled. "Does a man become any different when he puts on a gown?" Frankfurter asked himself in 1953. "I say," he replied somewhat self-consciously, "if he is any good, he does."[80] "We know," the *1956 Report of the American Bar Association's Committee on the Federal Judiciary* declared, "that when the American lawyer becomes a judge he can and almost invariably does throw off all partisan ties and prejudices."[81] Justice Black has suggested that it may be too late to keep alive the delusion that our government, thanks to judicial review, is a government of laws and not men. In the Dennis[82] case of 1950 he expressed the hope that "in calmer times, when present pressures, passions and fears subside, this or some later Court will restore the First Amendment liberties to the high preferred place where they belong in a free society."[83] Black thus arouses the very suspicion that Frankfurter is most anxious to allay —that judicial decisions reflect "time and circumstances."

[79] Richmond News Leader, Feb. 11, 1955, p. 14, col. 1, in 101 Cong. Rec. A-882 (1955) (extension of remarks of Representative Harrison).

[80] Frankfurter, Of Law and Men 133 (1956). Other judges, good ones, have not felt the transforming effects of a gown. "As one who is privileged to wear the judicial robe," former Justice Ferdinand Pecora of the New York Supreme Court commented in 1937,

> let me assure you that there is no magic in the robe. It does not invest its wearer with qualities he did not possess before the robe was draped about his shoulders. It does not endow him with an intellectuality or a spirituality not his previously. It does not transform his personality. It does not enable him to step out of that personality and assume a new one. If he lacked humanity before he donned the robe, his understanding is not leavened with that virtue by it.

Hearings on Reorganization of the Federal Judiciary before the Senate Committee on the Judiciary, 75th Cong., 1st Sess. 422–23 (1937).

The late Judge Jerome Frank believed that "much harm is done by the myth that, merely by putting on a black robe and taking the oath of office as a judge, a man ceases to be human and strips himself of all predilections, becomes a passionless thinking machine." Frank, *Preface* to Frank, Law and the Modern Mind at 7 (6th ed. 1949). See Frank, Courts on Trial, 1–4, 254–61, 310–15, 405–15, 427–29 (1949).

[81] 81 A.B.A. Rep. 438 (1956).

[82] Dennis v. United States, 341 U.S. 494 (1950).   [83] *Id.* at 581 (dissenting opinion).

What happens when the Court unflinchingly enters the political arena is illuminated by two historic examples—*Scott* v. *Sandford*[84] and *Brown* v. *Board of Educ.*[85] Separated by almost a century, the action in both cases was obviously in response to time and circumstances. "[T]here had become such a difference of opinion," said Justice Wayne in words as applicable in 1954 as they were in 1857, "that the peace and harmony of the country required the settlement of them by judicial decision."[86] In 1857 extension of slavery was a major issue; in 1954 racial discrimination was not only creating domestic unrest, but also projecting a highly unfavorable image of America to the entire world. In both instances, the Court attempted to settle a volcanic issue once and for all; in both, the opinions were less firmly grounded than seemed desirable in decisions so momentous. The Justices split nine ways in Dred Scott; in Brown they were unanimous, allowing Chief Justice Warren to throw the full weight of his office and the prestige of the Court behind a ruling certain to provoke bitter controversy. Taney and his quarrelsome majority denied Congress power it wanted to exert, an authority many felt it could properly exercise. Warren's Court, on the other hand, asserted a power which Congress, under existing Senate rules, could not use even if there had been the will to do so.[87] Taney raised an absolute bar against congressional action, ignoring precedents created by his own Court.[88] Though a line of decisions pointed in this direction,[89] Chief Justice Warren was careful not to overrule *Plessy* v. *Ferguson*[90] beyond the point necessary to abolish the "separate but equal" doctrine in the area of public education.

Certain commonplace lessons may be drawn from these explosive forays into judicial politics. Courts do not and cannot function in a vacuum; Supreme Court Justices may accelerate tendencies, but cannot reverse them. Chief Justice Taney declared that "any change in public opinion or feeling, in relation to this unfortunate race"[91] must under no circumstances be allowed to weigh in the balance. The Constitution "must be construed now as it was understood at the time of its adoption."[92] Chief Justice Warren was more realistic. In approaching racial segregation, the

---

[84] 60 U.S. (19 How.) 393 (1857).

[85] 347 U.S. 483 (1954).

[86] Scott v. Sandford, 60 U.S. (19 How.) 393, 454–55 (1857) (concurring opinion).

[87] Harris, *The Constitution, Education, and Segregation*, 29 TEMP. L.Q. 409 (1956).

[88] See CORWIN, THE DOCTRINE OF JUDICIAL REVIEW 134 (1914).

[89] See Missouri *ex rel.* Gaines v. Canada, 305 U.S. 337 (1938); Sipuel v. Board of Regents, 332 U.S. 631 (1948); Sweatt v. Painter, 339 U.S. 629 (1950); McLaurin v. Oklahoma State Regents, 339 U.S. 637 (1950).

[90] 163 U.S. 537 (1896).

[91] Scott v. Sandford, 60 U.S. (19 How.) 393, 426 (1857).

[92] *Ibid.*

Justices could not "turn the clock back to 1868 when the Amendment was adopted, or even to 1896 when *Plessy* v. *Ferguson* was written."[93] In both cases, the Court undertook to settle a seething issue beyond the capacity of any or all other agencies of government. One was an abortive endorsement of slavery, the other a furtherance of American ideals. In both instances the Court was criticized for making policy, for usurping the lawmaking function. Taney substituted his own conception of public policy for that declared by Congress. In 1954, Congress had not spoken on the subject of school desegregation. For practical reasons, implementation of the equal protection clause of the Fourteenth Amendment had been left to the Court.[94] Positive judicial responsibility had developed in this area. In 1857, Congress had acted; there was no need or justification for judicial policy-making. In 1954 there was every reason for it. The Court had written segregation into the Constitution. Under vastly changed circumstances, the Justices used their prerogative to read it out of our basic law.

The 1957–58 congressional attacks on the Warren Court illustrate the extent to which symbolism had been undermined.[95] Despite the apparent strength of its position, the Court's defenders were few compared to the number that rallied around the Hughes Court in 1937. At the peak of his power Franklin Roosevelt could muster the support of only twenty senators in favor of court-packing.[96] The Jenner-Butler bill went down in the Senate by the narrow margin of forty-nine to forty-one.[97] Roosevelt proposed to increase the Court's membership, leaving its power untouched. The recent proposals went far beyond these bounds. By withdrawing appellate jurisdiction in an important group of national security cases, they would have made the Court something less than supreme.

Why should popular protest against Roosevelt have been so spontaneous, and the Warren Court's outside support, including that of President Eisenhower,[98] so ambiguous? There are, of course, various possible

[93] Brown v. Board of Educ., 347 U.S. 483, 492 (1954).

[94] See Freund, *Storm over the American Supreme Court*, 21 MODERN L. REV. 345, 351 (1958).

[95] See generally MURPHY, CONGRESS AND THE COURT (1962).

[96] 81 CONG. REC. 7381 (1937) (vote to recommit bill to Committee on the Judiciary).

[97] 104 CONG. REC. 18687 (1958) (motion to table the bill).

[98] Asked at a news conference for an expression of opinion about the judicial order to desegregate, President Eisenhower was evasive. Any comment from him which might "weaken public opinion by discussion of separate cases, where I might agree or might disagree, seems to me to be completely unwise and not a good thing to do." PUBLIC PAPERS OF THE PRESIDENTS OF THE UNITED STATES, DWIGHT D. EISENHOWER (1958) 626 (1959). Compare Abraham Lincoln's words of June 26, 1857: "[W]e think the Dred Scott decision

reasons. One may be the inroads made since 1937 on the Court as a powerless emblem of justice. Judicial axioms of the most sacred character have been undermined: the mighty principle of *stare decisis* has been rudely shaken; the notion that sociological and other extralegal data are meet for legislatures but not for courts has been ignored; the venerable maxim, always tenuous, that courts exercise judgment and not will has been honored more in the breach than in the observance. Chief Justice Warren himself has slighted our legendary jurisprudence. "Our judges are not monks or scientists," the Chief Justice wrote in 1955, "but participants in the living stream of our national life, steering the law between the dangers of rigidity on the one hand and of formlessness on the other.[99]

Destruction of magic and other practices of witchcraft is a calculated risk. "Without a constant and sincere pursuit of the shining but never completely attainable ideal of the rule of law above men . . .," Thurman Arnold writes, "we would not have a civilized government. If that ideal be an illusion, to dispel it would cause men to lose themselves in an even greater illusion, the illusion that personal power can be benevolently exercised."[100] To regard the Court merely as an instrument of power might limit its effectiveness. Judicial decisions have been rendered more acceptable because of the belief that the Justices merely pronounce the law, deciding nothing. Nine men are more vulnerable than "the law" or "the Constitution." Candor, combined with a knowledge of unconcealed judicial disagreements, tends to rob the "higher law" of its dogmatic quality. Walter Bagehot reminds us that those elements in the governing process which "excite the most easy reverence" are "theatrical elements. . . . that which is mystic in its claims; that which is occult in its mode of action."[101]

Myth is a recognized adjunct to the governing process. Resort to it need not be blameworthy. It may merely reflect an honest mind trying to work out a highly intricate problem, or to explain a complicated truth.[102] The Janus-like role of the Supreme Court maximizes rather than diminishes its effectiveness. "The art of free society," Alfred North Whitehead has observed,

consists first in the maintenance of the symbolic code; and secondly in fearlessness of revision, to secure that the code serves those purposes which satisfy

---

is erroneous. We know that the court that made it has often overruled its own decisions, and we shall do what we can to have it overrule this." Quoted in 2 BEVERIDGE, ABRAHAM LINCOLN 511 (1928).

[99] Warren, *The Law and the Future*, Fortune, Nov. 1955, p. 107.

[100] Arnold, *Professor Hart's Theology*, 73 HARV. L. REV. 1298, 1311 (1960).

[101] BAGEHOT, THE ENGLISH CONSTITUTION AND OTHER POLITICAL ESSAYS 76 (rev. ed. 1872).

[102] See comment of Bishop James Pike in N.Y. Times, Feb. 13, 1961, p. 28, col. 1.

an enlightened reason. Those societies which cannot combine reverence to their symbols with freedom of revision must ultimately decay either from anarchy, or from the slow atrophy of a life stifled by useless shadows.[103]

All peoples respond, more or less, to political ritual. But Americans seem less dependent on it than the British. Before he was himself among the anointed, Felix Frankfurter believed that "it is not good, either for the country or the Court, that the part played by the Court in the life of the country should be shrouded in mystery. . . . 'The time is past, in the history of the world,' " he then thought, " 'when any living man or body of men can be set on a pedestal and decorated with a halo.' "[104] Yet it has been suggested that the Court's work requires "a degree of privacy incomparably stricter than is fitting in the legislative or executive process."[105]

Nothing of the sort was envisioned by the framers of the Constitution. Implicit in the system of government they designed is the basic premise that unchecked power in any hands whatsoever is intolerable. Only that power which is recognized can be effectively limited. In 1956, when nearly one hundred Southern congressmen issued a manifesto calling for reversal of the segregation decisions by "lawful means," eminent lawyers condemned the manifesto as "reckless."[106] Refusal to obey any Supreme Court mandate is, of course, intolerable. But to deny, or even question, the right of those who disagree with it to seek change by "lawful means" appears not in keeping with the principles of a free society.

Should Lincoln have been muzzled for his attack on the Dred Scott decision? After the Supreme Court had on two occasions outlawed child labor legislation as beyond the reach of congressional authority, should the efforts of those who deplored this impasse as unnecessary have been stayed? Consistent with the opprobrium heaped on the heads of those who criticized the Court's desegregation decision, President Roosevelt should have been impeached for his ill-tempered press conference denouncing the unanimous Schechter[107] decision as carrying us back to the "horse and buggy" days. Surely criticism must not be confined to those

---

[103] Whitehead, Symbolism—Its Meaning and Effect 88 (1927).

[104] Frankfurter, *The Supreme Court and the Public*, 83 Forum 329–30, 334 (1930).

[105] Bickel, *The Court: An Indictment Analyzed*, N.Y. Times, April 27, 1958, § 6 (Magazine), p. 16, 64. See Cahn, *Eavesdropping on Justice*, The Nation, Jan. 5, 1957, p. 14. Before becoming a Supreme Court Justice, Professor Frankfurter regretted that "intimacies of the conference room—the workshop of the living Constitution" should be denied the historian. Frankfurter, The Commerce Clause under Marshall, Taney, and Waite 9 (1937).

[106] See N.Y. Times, Oct. 28, 1956, p. 63, col. 1.

[107] A. L. A. Schechter Poultry Corp. v. United States, 295 U.S. 495 (1935).

decisions which happen to run counter to our own tightly held preferences. "One may criticize," as Holmes says, "even what one reveres."[108]

Suspicion of an inconsistency between a non-elective, non-removable, and potentially powerful Court, and a government deriving its powers from the consent of the governed, has always been a gnawing, tantalizing concern. The Supreme Court poses the impasse Samuel Seabury noted nearly two centuries ago: "No scheme of human policy can be so contrived and guarded, but that something must be left to the integrity, prudence, and wisdom of those who govern."[109] The electorate, through its chosen representatives, can make the government conform to its will. But the Constitution sets limits, enforceable by nine politically non-responsible men. The dilemma was once resolved by recourse to the fiction that the Court has no power; it merely applies the Constitution which, in some mystical way, is always the highest expression of the people's will. Though this ancient theory still has vitality, it is not altogether satisfying. The occult aspect of the judging process has evoked critical comment from judges themselves. Learned Hand noted:

[J]udges are seldom content merely to annul the particular solution before them; they do not, indeed they may not, say that taking all things into consideration, the legislators' solution is too strong for the judicial stomach. On the contrary they wrap up their veto in a protective veil of adjectives such as "arbitrary," "artificial," "normal," "reasonable," "inherent," "fundamental," or "essential," whose office usually, though quite innocently, is to disguise what they are doing and impute to it a derivation far more impressive than their personal preferences, which are all that in fact lie behind the decision. If we do need a third chamber it should appear for what it is, and not as the interpreter of inscrutable principles.[110]

To command public confidence and respect, judicial authority need not be transcendent, awe-inspiring, immune to criticism—screened from the public eye. The Court's firm command over the hearts and minds of men is not grounded in mystery, but in the contemplative pause and the sober second thought its restraining power entails. Judicial control is facilitated by precept and example. Decisions based on reason and authority have a moral force far exceeding that of the purse or the sword. The judicial process requires the articulation of ideals and values that might otherwise be silenced. In passing judgment on living issues, in resolving disputes which are at any given moment puzzling and dividing us, the Court teaches the demanding lesson of free government.

[108] HOLMES, *The Path of the Law*, in COLLECTED LEGAL PAPERS 194 (1920).

[109] PUBLICATIONS OF THE WESTCHESTER COUNTY HISTORICAL SOCIETY, No. VIII, LETTERS OF A WESTCHESTER FARMER 121 (1930).

[110] HAND, THE BILL OF RIGHTS 70 (1958).

BENJAMIN F. WRIGHT

The Southern Political Tradition

THERE ARE two lines of inquiry to be pursued in dealing with the subject of this paper. First: Is there *a* Southern political tradition, or should the question be stated in the plural? Is there, that is to say, more than one tradition associated with the South? Second: What is the nature of this tradition, or of these traditions? The most satisfactory introduction to this double-barreled question is, I think, to be found in the views of two of the leading historians of the South. Both have written excellent essays on the factors which give to the South its distinctive character, its identity as a section. These essays are to be found in Professor C. Vann Woodward's *The Burden of Southern History*,[1] and Professor T. Harry Williams' *Romance and Realism in Southern Politics*.[2]

Neither of these scholars bases his identification of the South on the characteristics most familiar to popular history and journalism: the climate, the one-horse farm, one-crop agriculture, the sharecropper, one-party politics, the poll tax, Jim Crow, lynching, the white primary. These, other than climate, are gone or on the way out. Mr. Woodward notes that the South is going through the process of economic development that the North and East experienced a generation or more ago, and going through it more rapidly. Both the delay and the speed help to explain several aspects of economics, politics, and labor relations in the South.

While the race problem continues in the South, it is equally true that significant changes have taken and are taking place. It is also evident that there has recently been a very considerable migration of Negroes from South to North and West and that problems of race are increasingly evident in New York, Chicago, Detroit, and Los Angeles, in scores of suburbs, and in such small-city welfare controversies as that in New-

BENJAMIN F. WRIGHT is Professor of Government at the University of Texas.

[1] Baton Rouge: Louisiana State University Press, 1960.

[2] Athens: University of Georgia Press, 1961.

burgh, New York. The race problem is Southern; it is also national and almost universal.

What is most distinctive about the South, says Professor Woodward, and with this view Professor Williams differs only in emphasis, is its history, its "collective experience." For a long period the South was poor. Professor David Potter has argued convincingly that a major factor in shaping America is that it has been a land of plenty.[3] Of course, this is not just a matter of natural resources. The soil, the timber, the water, the minerals—all these and other resources were here for centuries before the European settlements, but the Indians never became "a people of plenty." It is, however, incontestably true that over a period of several generations the per capita wealth of the South was far below that in the North.

The American legend of success and invincibility, of never knowing defeat in war, is not shared by the South. The South had the experience of "frustration, failure and defeat," as well as government under alien control after that defeat.

One does not have to accept a ridiculously erroneous view that the North, the East, and the West have no sins of record, no history of exploitation of labor, of denial to old citizens and new immigrants of essential rights, in order to agree with Professor Woodward that the South is unique in the extent of time that it lived with the evil of slavery, and that this continued for over a generation after slavery was, elsewhere in the Christian world, accepted as evil. The colonies which became the United States, unlike the French in the St. Lawrence Valley or the Spanish in Latin America, never had to break with feudalism. They were spared that heritage from medieval Europe, but they were not spared a heritage of imported slavery, though only in the South did this institution survive into the nineteenth century.

All of this is substantially accurate and definitely important. What it largely ignores is the South of the seventeenth and eighteenth centuries, and especially that magnificent flowering that began about 1760 and continued into the nineteenth century. Professors Woodward and Williams are writing about the South as though its history began around 1831. Is that *the* Old South, or are there at least two Old Souths, the first and older South being one that was, in decisive respects, different from "the South as a Conscious Minority"?[4] Before about 1828 the South was a clearly marked section, as was New England. There were episodes, as in the Federal Convention of 1787, when representatives

[3] *People of Plenty* (Chicago: University of Chicago Press, 1954).

[4] See Jesse T. Carpenter, *The South as a Conscious Minority* (New York: New York University Press, 1930). Though dealing with the entire period 1789–1861, the author is principally concerned with the last three or four decades of this era.

of the South proclaimed its identity as a section, but none equaled the spectacular character of the Hartford Convention in 1814. In this period the South was not isolated; it was not poor; it had not known defeat; it was not frustrated; and it provided, in the years before and during the Revolution, as well as in the Constitutional Convention and the first four decades under the Constitution, a major share of the nation's leaders. To this great period in the history of the South I shall return after discussing three political writers of what is usually known as the Old South: John Taylor of Caroline, John C. Calhoun, and George Fitzhugh.

The first of them is a transitional figure. John Taylor of Caroline County, Virginia, died in 1824, when Calhoun was still a nationalist, thirty years before Fitzhugh published his first book. His books have relatively little to say about the South's "peculiar institution" (slavery) for the simple reason that the controversy over slavery was not the central issue during his lifetime. But from the Revolution, when first he became attached to the state-rights cause, to 1824, he was the most voluminous, if not the most eloquent, defender of the state-rights, sectional, agrarian creed. With the possible exception of John Marshall, one of his frequent targets, he was the most consistent. He began his writings under the influence of Patrick Henry during the Revolution and in the controversy over ratification of the Constitution in 1787–88. When Patrick Henry went over to the Federalist party after 1789, and was even offered appointment as Chief Justice of the United States by Washington, Taylor continued to preach the gospel of local self-rule. He was more Jeffersonian than Jefferson in the debates of the 1790's when the issues were the Hamiltonian finance system, the tariff, internal improvements, and always, directly or indirectly, agrarianism. He was first, last, all the time, for his state, his section, his way of life as a planter. He served in the Senate of the United States three times, though briefly each time, and he seemed never to be at home there.

It is in his pamphlets and his books, not in his rare speeches, that he expounded his Jeffersonian, or, more accurately, his anti-Federalist doctrine, for, unlike Jefferson's, Taylor's writings are almost exclusively in opposition. Of constructive doctrine there is very little.[5] The anonymous *Definition of Parties* published in 1794 is an all-out attack on the financial program of Hamilton as one "for the exclusive benefit" of the

[5] In my essay on Taylor written 36 years ago, "The Philosopher of Jeffersonian Democracy," *American Political Science Review*, XXII (1928), 870, I failed to distinguish between the inflexible localism and essential conservatism of Taylor and the optimistic democracy of Jefferson. They were, as the latter once said, almost always together in political controversies after 1789, but the contrast between their basic philosophies is as great as it is significant of the relevance of each for the present day. For a longer account of his writings see Eugene T. Mudge, *The Social Philosophy of John Taylor of Caroline* (New York: Columbia University Press, 1939).

money—or as he calls it, the "paper-interest." It will benefit the 5,000 at the expense of the 5,000,000. It will create a paper aristocracy enriching a few in New York and Massachusetts. Land is, he says, the only natural source of wealth; it is "natural property" as distinguished from "political property" of paper. The "stock-jobbing interest" is taking over and the cause of representative government is in danger. A system of "privileged orders" is put in its place.

In Taylor's first, and shortest book, which has the unusual but not inappropriate title of *Arator*,[6] he defends an agricultural economy, especially that of the South, against manufacturing, the (discriminatory) tariff, the national bank—all of which he designates as methods of "rendering governments too strong for nations." If agriculture, which, along with politics, is the true source of the wealth of nations, be required to pay bounties to manufacturing, both economic health and political liberty will be lost. He reflects a late eighteenth-century, rather than a post-1831, view to the extent that he sees slavery as a misfortune to agriculture. He believes, however, that it is capable only of amelioration, not removal. He disagrees with Jefferson, criticizing the latter's harsh condemnation of slavery and "slave holders" in his *Notes on Virginia*. Given the circumstances which exist, including the moral inferiority of the Negroes, emancipation is impossible.

Between 1814 and 1823 Taylor published four large books, the first being *An Inquiry into the Principles and Policy of the Government of the United States* (1814). It is an attack, long after the event, upon the theories of John Adams' *Defence of the Constitutions* and *The Federalist*, both of course dating back to the 1786–88 era. His *Construction Construed and Constitutions Vindicated* (1820) deals with two very recent matters, for it is a condemnation of Marshall's opinion in *M'Culloch* v. *Maryland* (1819) and the Missouri Compromise. His *Tyranny Unmasked* (1822) is the longest critique of the protectionist tariff policy. His *New Views of the Constitution of the United States* (1823) was his final blast in support of state rights. Had Taylor's *Inquiry* appeared in 1788, rather than in 1814, it might have attracted more attention, provided he were less prolix and able to write with some measure of grace and eloquence. John Randolph, in a letter to a friend, once wrote, "For heaven's sake, get some worthy person to do the second edition into *English*." There was no second edition, not, that is, for 136 years. The Yale University Press reprinted it in 1950. The three books of his old age are all equally difficult to read; he makes no concessions to the reader. What is lacking is the eloquence of Burke, or the clarity and conciseness of Madison, or the superb style of Calhoun at his best. The three last books, unlike

[6] Published in 1803. It was his most popular work. Six editions were published by 1819. See especially pp. 5–16, 19–22, 48–55, 90–101, 218–20.

the *Inquiry*, were very much related to current controversy, but Taylor was no phrase-maker, no master of the art of enlisting support by the use of words and slogans that appeal both to the mind and the emotions; so too he published before the South became passionately, single-mindedly devoted to its, by that time, "peculiar institution" and to every aspect of life—economics, politics, art and letters, legend and myth—believed to be connected with slavery. It remained for others, some years after Taylor's death, to become the accepted defenders of what is usually meant by the term "the Old South."

Taylor, though a loyal, zealous, and consistent state righter, a plantation- and slaveowner, lived and wrote when the South was still an organic part of the Union. While he was writing his books which expounded the gospel of state rights and sectionalism, Calhoun of South Carolina was a nationalist, at times an advocate of national aid to internal improvements, and even of a tariff. Then came the change-over. Calhoun's views changed because, as he interpreted the course of events, the interests of his state and his section changed. He was, in his opinion, as much the spokesman for the South before 1825 as after 1828. First came the fight against the tariff. The climax of this controversy took place when South Carolina attempted to nullify an act of Congress, an attempt vigorously opposed by the aged James Madison, author of the Virginia Resolution of 1799,[7] and thwarted by President Andrew Jackson, born in North Carolina, elected from Tennessee. In defense of his stand on nullification Calhoun wrote and spoke with a clarity, an eloquence, and a force never attained by Taylor. Even the "South Carolina Exposition" and the speeches in defense of that position do not reflect the fully developed theory of this extraordinary man, one who would have been a great national figure, perhaps the one truly significant political philosopher to come out of the United States in the nineteenth century, had it not been for the march of events which caused him, and his state, to assume an uncompromisingly defensive and negative position.

The Old South, in the usual stereotype, begins not with the introduction of slavery early in the seventeenth century, or with the Revolution, or with opposition to the Hamiltonian financial policies. Before 1831, to select one highly significant illustration, there were more antislavery societies in the South than in the North. Indeed, most of the enlightened critics of slavery were in the South.[8]

Usually it is an oversimplification to give a specific date for the beginning of a major movement of thought and feeling. Certainly anti-slavery sentiment did not originate in 1831. There is, however, some

[7] Irving Brant, *James Madison*, VI: *James Madison, Commander in Chief, 1812–1836* (Indianapolis and New York: Bobbs-Merrill, 1961), 468–500, 512, 531.

[8] Williams, *op. cit.*, pp. 8–11.

point in selecting January 1, 1831, as the date for the beginning of the abolitionist crusade, for on that day appeared the first number of William Lloyd Garrison's *Liberator*, with its declaration of intent to wage a relentless battle for immediate emancipation. Later in the same year came the Nat Turner slave rebellion which resulted in the death of some sixty white persons; this intensified the fear of other such "rebellions" and increased Southern hatred of the abolitionists who, many believed, were partly responsible for Nat Turner's revolt. This is not the place to give due credit to the egoism, the lack of balance and of simple common sense, involved in a campaign for immediate abolition. The hearts of the abolitionists may have been pure, but they made one of the classic, tragic mistakes of history when they sought immediate abolition of the ancient and deeply entrenched and enmeshed system of chattel slavery. What they lacked was wisdom, as well as compassion for those who inherited the institution of slavery, the kind of perspective judgment which considers the side-effects of an instantaneous break with the past. Nor can I here stop to pay an overdue tribute to the dangerous superficiality or the inconsistency of Thoreau's *Civil Disobedience*, or to the outrageous support given to the fanatic John Brown after his capture and conviction for attempting to initiate a slave rebellion—support by people who, through native intelligence, education, the study of history, should have realized how terrible would be the results of a slave insurrection.[9] Brown was not a suitable subject for woolly sentimentality. Support for him, after Harpers Ferry, by the eminent and highly respectable is a perfect example of worthy ends made ignoble by utterly false means.

There are many ifs, none provable, about the coming of the War for Southern Independence. Could it have been avoided if slavery had been prohibited in the new Southwest, as it was in the Northwest Territory? If the slave trade had been prohibited (and the prohibition enforced) in 1789? If the abolitionists had never been born? If the South had ignored the abolitionist attacks? By the time of John Brown it may have been an irresistible conflict. I do not know. We do know that we fought the bloodiest war of the nineteenth century, a war in which everyone except a few profiteers lost, in order to resolve that conflict. I can think of no procedure better calculated to wreck the economy of the South and to render particularly harsh the position of the Negroes.

By 1831 almost every civilized country had abolished slavery within its borders, and most had done so in their colonies, as Britain was about to do in the West Indies. In the American South slavery was a social blight and an economic liability except in some of the newer plantation areas. Almost certainly it was doomed to extinction by one of several

[9] Woodward, *op. cit.*, chap. 3, esp. pp. 49 ff.

processes within a generation. But the fanatical abolitionist attack helped the South to make nearly every possible mistake.[10] It identified its entire way of life with this evil and out-of-date institution. Within a few years it was unsafe to condemn slavery as, for instance, the great Virginia landowner and slaveowner, and author of the first state constitution and bill of rights, George Mason, had done in 1787. It was both safe and popular to repudiate Jefferson and all his supposed egalitarian theories. The freedom of thought and expression, so cherished by the great men of the Revolution and the constitutional era, when debate was an accepted essential of life, no longer existed. The South even alienated its "natural ally, the West," by insisting that the West accept its position on slavery in the territories, where, in most places, slavery could not be established.[11]

With this less than dispassionate preamble let me turn to the colossus of Southern political theory, John C. Calhoun of South Carolina.

Calhoun was, of course, not the first to write and speak in defense of slavery and the slave economy. Others did so before 1831, and the reaction to the abolitionist attack, and to the Nat Turner slave rebellion, came quickly. Debates of the kind held in the Virginia legislature of 1831–32, in which the proslavery party won, but not overwhelmingly, became impossible. Instead we have speeches and writings such as the tract of Professor Thomas R. Dew of the College of William and Mary in which he condemned the members of that legislature who even questioned that "slavery was established and sanctioned by divine authority" or that it lessened the "cruelties of war," or claimed that it was in any way "unfavorable to a republican spirit."[12] In brief, Professor Dew declared that slavery, as well as the system of which it is an essential element, is based upon divine and natural law, is justified by history, and is one of the chief supports of a popular government.

Similar, and not less emphatic, defenses of slave society are found in many of Calhoun's papers in the thirties and later. Thus, in his "Speech on the Reception of the Abolition Petitions" in the Senate, February 6, 1837,[13] he insists that the white and black races have lived in peace and happiness and that never before has the Negro race "attained a condition so civilized and so improved, not only physically, but morally and intellectually." The white people of the South have "contributed our full share of talents and political wisdom in forming and sustaining this political fabric . . . [have been] constantly inclined most strongly

[10] Williams, *op. cit.*, p. 10.

[11] *Ibid.*, p. 12.

[12] Dew's "Review of the Debate . . ." (1833) was reprinted in *The Pro-Slavery Argument*, by Lippincott in Philadelphia in 1853. The quotations are from pp. 293 ff., 461.

[13] *Works of John C. Calhoun*, ed. R. K. Crallé (New York: Appleton, 1853), II, 630–33.

to the side of liberty. . . . In one thing only are we inferior—the arts of gain; we acknowledge that we are less wealthy than the Northern section of the Union, but I trace this mainly to the fiscal action of this Government which has extracted much from, and spent little among us." Failure to industrialize he does not mention. What he does assert is that slavery is a positive good for the black race, especially when compared to the condition and hardships of white laborers in the industrial countries of Europe and the North. He had a point there, though it did not justify the continuance of slavery.

A year later, in a Senate debate, he admitted that many in the South "once believed that it [slavery] was a moral and political evil." The abolitionist "agitation" has "produced one happy effect"; it has compelled the South to "look into the nature and character of this great institution," to correct such erroneous views, and to see that slavery is natural, salutary, productive of harmony, union, stability, conservatism unknown in the "less fortunately constituted" North where the conflict between capital and labor is "constantly on the increase."[14]

When Calhoun died in 1850 he left unpublished, though almost completed, two treatises which were the literary and philosophical product of his twenty years' fight for slave society and state sovereignty. The *Disquisition on Government* and the *Discourse on the Constitution and Government of the United States* were published shortly after his death.[15] They are far from negligible yet, as I have indicated, they are primarily monuments to an impressive talent which was devoted to a losing, because a backward-looking, cause. In them, there is verbal loyalty to the Virginia and Kentucky Resolutions of 1798 and 1799, but the spirit of Jefferson and Madison is missing. The defense of the rights of free speech and a free press, of adaptation to changing circumstances, of the broadening of power and privilege, of a vision of a greater future—all is gone. There is much about the dangers of majority rule and about an elaborate structure for protecting minority rights, but the minority is not man, or men: it is a geographical section. His theoretical defense of the principle of concurrent majority is no more than the right of a minority group of states, even of one state, to block, or to veto, laws passed by the federal Congress. It is not a sophomoric proposal, as was Thoreau's *Civil Disobedience*, but if put into effect, it would be almost equally effective in rendering inoperable a system of representative government under a written constitution. His only concession to the unworkability of nullification is that if three-fourths of the states support the action of the government (a vote to be taken by the state legisla-

---

[14] *Ibid.*, III, 179–81.

[15] These make up Vol. I of the Crallé edition of his *Works*.

tures; in the meantime the act of Congress would be in abeyance!), the minority state must yield *or* withdraw from the Union. To this extreme has the defense of the morally indefensible institution of the South carried one of the most powerful minds of nineteenth-century America.

Calhoun appears to me to be a truly tragic figure. He should have been as splendid a leader for the future of his state, his section, his nation as had been Washington, Jefferson, Madison, Marshall, or, for that matter, his contemporary, Jackson, but the fates decreed otherwise. He saw his role as leader in a cause which we today know to have been lost before it was undertaken. The aftermath of that cause was the retention of a defeatist attitude after the War for Southern Independence was ended, after General Lee had turned his great talents, as president of little Washington College, toward regaining the position in the nation which the South had once held.

Before I turn to the post-1865 era, let me write more briefly than I should wish about one other political theorist who wrote in defense of slavery and of Southern society in the 1850's. I cannot regard George Fitzhugh of Virginia as a tragic figure. Neither is he a comic character. He could never, so far as I know him and his writings, have become a national leader. He did have something of importance to say, though he mixed that with remarks and doctrines verging on the ridiculous. He was a man of little formal education, though of wide, if not very discriminate reading. His *Sociology for the South* (1854) and his *Cannibals All* (1857), as well as his many articles, especially in *De Bow's Review*, offer not only a defense of slavery and slave society but also an unqualified, a biting, in many ways a trenchant, attack upon the inherent defects, or, more accurately, the existing sins, of free society. Where most of what Calhoun and Dew wrote on slavery is as dead as that institution, much of Fitzhugh's critique of free and competitive society has relevance for our times. He was wordy, discursive, sometimes inconsistent, ignorant of much that he should have known, extravagant in some arguments, but he wrote with cogency and force of the indisputable mistakes and evils of early industrialism. He did point out flaws with which succeeding generations struggled and are still struggling. We cannot agree that the best of all possible institutions for civilized society is slavery, nor that "our only quarrel with socialism is that it will not honestly admit that it owes its recent revival to the failure of universal liberty," though we can agree that communism (also called socialism by the Russians) "is seeking to bring about slavery again in some form."[16]

Where Calhoun's formidable books are based in good part upon a legalistic interpretation of state rights, Fitzhugh professes to be con-

[16] *Sociology for the South*, p. 70.

cerned for the interests of the weak and powerless persons, to be against a code of "simple and unadulterated selfishness," to be in harmony with the New Testament principles of self-denial, brotherliness, of community rather than war in the bosom of society. Only under slavery are the weak provided for, not according to their wealth but according to their needs.[17] Liberty, he argues, is not a good but is an evil. The object of government is to correct this evil. No man is born free. All government is slavery.[18]

It is necessary to ignore the absurd in his books, but, I repeat, his relevance is not only to the social system which was outlawed by the Thirteenth Amendment. He does expose weaknesses and defects of the early laissez faire society; he does advocate care for the weak and the helpless. He also advocates diversification of the Southern economy. The profits from agriculture, he asserts, are only a third of those from commerce and manufacturing.[19] The final and conclusive weakness of an agrarian economy is the "intellectual superiority of all other pursuits over agriculture."[20]

Fitzhugh's interest in a higher standard of intellectual life than the one then existing in the South is reflected in his advocacy of a much-improved school system, especially of free schools for the poorer whites. He did not agree with Jefferson's ideal of liberty, but he did go along with the earlier Virginian on the importance of both schools and news-papers: the wide circulation of newspapers is essential to public enlightenment.[21]

The experience of turning from the writings of Taylor, Calhoun, and Fitzhugh to a search for evidence of a Southern political tradition in the decades after the War is as intellectually disappointing as it is emotionally distressing—at least to one whose forebears lived in the South.

Some of the more recent histories of Reconstruction give a less unhappy picture of government in the South than that I acquired as a small boy from my ex-Confederate grandfathers. With the accuracy of either picture I am not here concerned. For present purposes it is not important to know how many Negroes there were in state offices or what was the proportion of carpetbaggers to scalawags (apparently there were many more of the latter than of the former). I do think it relevant to state that the attempt to give the suffrage immediately, without time for education, to a primitive, illiterate, newly freed people was as unwise as it was, in the outcome, unfortunate for the Negroes. But then, calm and informed judgments were not characteristics of the Reconstruction policy after Lincoln's death.

[17] *Ibid.*, pp. 245 ff.

[18] *Ibid.*, p. 170.

[19] *Ibid.*, pp. 46, 158.

[20] *Ibid.*, p. 17.

[21] *Ibid.*, p. 146.

During Reconstruction the South was even more distinctly set off from the remainder of the nation than it was between 1831 and 1861. Even after the formal end of Reconstruction in 1877, it was set apart by poverty, by low standards of living, by the prevalence of violence, by absence of diversity in the economy, and by the migration of much of its talent and energy to the North or West.

Professor Woodward estimates that the South's share of the $47,642,-000,000 value of property in the nation in 1877 was but $5,725,000,000. The per capita wealth was $376 as compared with $1,086 in the other states.[22] The per capita wealth of Virginia, richest state in the South, was not within $100 of that in Kansas, the poorest non-Southern state. What Fitzhugh had written about the rewards of exclusive agriculture was all too clearly supported by these statistics.

The South of this era enjoyed the greatest incidence of violence and of homicide, and not only in the black belts. The statistics are appalling to one who sees in law enforcement a major indication of the advance of civilization. This is true not only when the figures for the South are compared with those for the North. Italy, with the highest homicide rate in Europe, had fewer convicts charged with this crime than had the South Central States, though Italy had over three times the population to draw on. "The South seems to have been one of the most violent communities of comparable size in all Christendom."[23]

Of even greater importance for the future of the South was the flight of talent, the departure of young men of unusual ability for a career in the North or West. The foremost architect of his day, H. H. Richardson, left New Orleans for the North, as did the Georgia-born architect, John Wellborn Root. Joseph and John Le Conte were other Georgians who won fame as scientists in California; there was no place for them at home. Many examples of this loss of ability and ambition could be given. None is more pertinent to the present inquiry than the story of Woodrow Wilson, born in Virginia, with a boyhood spent largely in Augusta, Georgia, and Columbia, South Carolina, a graduate of the University of Virginia Law School, who practiced for a time in Atlanta. His mother's family ties were with the latter two states, and Wilson married Ellen Axson of Rome, Georgia. Moreover, he had gone to Atlanta with high hopes because he thought it a city rapidly emerging from the exhaustion of war and the troubles of Reconstruction, and because he thought "a man's mind may be expected to grow most freely

[22] C. Vann Woodward, *Origins of the New South, 1877–1913* (Baton Rouge: Louisiana State University Press, 1951), pp. 110–11.

[23] *Ibid.*, p. 159.

in its native air."[24] The ties of ancestry, of boyhood, of law school, and of marriage, like the hopes, were not enough. In 1883 he wrote that "the studious man is pronounced impractical and is suspected as a visionary." The career of this spendid scholar, teacher, university president, governor, and President was to lie in the North. Had he remained in the South, he would probably never have gained national, much less international, stature. Nor would he have had the opportunity to bring Southern men, both those who had gone North for a career (McAdoo, McReynolds, Walter Hines Page) or those who remained in the South (Daniels and Burleson) to his cabinet, or to high diplomatic or other national offices.

The years from 1877 to 1913 do not constitute an inspiring period to recall. In spite of many, and often eloquent, speeches by Henry W. Grady and others on the "New South," it appears evident that the South had not recovered its old distinction or its onetime intellectual eminence or, as indicated above, a degree of economic prosperity comparable to that of other sections. The late James W. Garner, native of Mississippi, graduate of Mississippi State College, but for thirty-four years head of the department of political science at the University of Illinois, summed up the situation *before* 1861:

Of the fifteen Presidents of the United States elected between 1789 and 1861, a period of seventy-two years, nine came from the South, and the aggregate of their terms of service amounted to nearly fifty years. Of the fourteen Vice-Presidents, six came from the South; of the thirty-seven Justices of the Supreme Court appointed during this period, twenty-nine were Southern men; of the one hundred and fifty-three cabinet officers, seventy-three were from the Southern states; of the twenty-three speakers of the national house of representatives, twelve were Southern men; and so were forty-seven of the eighty-two diplomatic representatives accredited to the courts of England, France, Austria, Russia, and Spain.[25]

After the war, and until 1913, the only Southerner in the Presidency was Andrew Johnson. Only fourteen of one hundred and thirty-three cabinet members were from the South, only seven of the thirty-one Justices of the Supreme Court, and two of the twelve Speakers of the House. None of the Southern senators approached the position of eminence and influence held by many before 1861. As Professor Woodward puts it, "Never in the history of the country, and rarely in the history of any country, had there been a comparable shift in the geography of political power."[26]

[24] Ray Stannard Baker, *Woodrow Wilson, Life and Letters* (New York: Doubleday, Page, 1927), I, 139–40.

[25] "Southern Politics since the Civil War," in *Studies in Southern History and Politics* (New York: Columbia University Press, 1914), p. 370.

[26] *Origins of the New South*, pp. 456–57.

How many "mute inglorious Miltons," how many potential Marshalls or Madisons or Pinckneys or Rutledges or Iredells or Calhouns or Jacksons were denied the opportunity for intellectual growth and for recognition and national leadership because of the poverty, the educational backwardness, the obsession with the Lost Cause, I do not know. But whether we read of the redeemers who rescued the South from the depths of Reconstruction, or the Populist leaders of the eighties and nineties, the emphasis is so heavily local that it is not easy to see them in the seats of the Founders. Of course, the quality of politics and of political thinking in the North was not of the 1776 or 1787 standard. Far from it. There had not been so dreary or so mediocre a period since Jamestown was settled. It was an era when the rapidity of economic and social change far outstripped political thinking or the quality of official political leadership. Even in those conditions the standards of politics in the South were not notable.

Unfortunately for the South, which embraced the movement more heartily than did even the West, the Populist movement did not live up to its possibilities or its promises. The South needed, and needed badly, a new birth of spirit and enterprise, of enlisting government not to check the growth of the economy and of education, but to encourage and abet them. The flight of talent to the North and West continued at a time when persons of exceptional ability and energy were badly needed in the South.

The South possesses the two oldest state universities (Georgia and North Carolina) and the second oldest independent college (William and Mary), but in this era they and other Southern colleges and universities were left far behind by the growth in quality of both independent and state institutions of North and West. The effects of that age of poverty, neglect, and low aims are still seen throughout the South, as a recent speech by Dean Heard of the University of North Carolina Graduate School makes clear.[27]

This reference to the standing of institutions of higher learning in the South is not just a reflection of professional interest. The lack of deep concern and respect for scientific and humanistic learning in the South not only reflects its poverty in the half-century after Reconstruction but also the quality of its political thought. We may, and should, assume that far too many of the South's ablest young men, who might have led their section back to its onetime position in the nation, were killed or crippled fighting in the armies of the Confederacy. But what of the next group, those like Woodrow Wilson (born in 1856), who were too young to take part in that conflict? It is symbolic of the era that the young Wilson, who at first eagerly threw in his lot with the South, soon gave

[27] *New York Times*, January 14, 1962.

up and moved to Johns Hopkins, to Princeton, and then, by way of the governorship of New Jersey, to the White House. My guess is that there were far more stories, either of migration to the North or of inability to make a career worthy of the section's earlier traditions, than the South could afford.

One of the reasons for the standards of too many of the leaders of the Populist movement in the South, and of some of its unhappy by-products, was the absence of adequate education of the leaders, an education which might have helped provide the vision and the perspective worthy of the needs and the opportunities. To be sure, the poverty and negligible education of a large proportion of their constituents were a tremendous handicap. Whatever the reasons, this attempt to bring together the farmers and laborers did little for the most needy groups in the South, less for the general development of its economy, and was positively detrimental to the growth of an attitude toward the race question—that issue which had obscured other major problems for two generations.[28] The Bourbons, as the historians call them, who largely controlled political office after Reconstruction, were not believers in the equality of the races, but it was the Populist leaders who, depending primarily upon the intensely race-conscious small farmers, found themselves running on white-supremacy tickets and appealing to the least literate and most reactionary part of the electorate. Popular democracy did not show up well in these campaigns. Instead of frank and open discussion of racial feelings and the resulting problems, the Populist candidates often outbid each other in denouncing Yankees and Negroes, along with the rich and powerful in the South. They sometimes sounded radical. In fact, they did not threaten the old order. What was too often present was that most unfortunate kind of scapegoatism which helped intensify the difficulties of a race problem already difficult enough. To a later generation was left a heritage of bad laws and worse feelings.

Incidentally, it seems improbable that the race problem, whether in New York or Mississsippi or Detroit or the exurbanite communities of the big cities, is capable of final solution in the immediate future. It is our version of an almost universal problem, and it will be with us for an indefinite time.[29] But the South, like New York, Chicago, and Detroit, has other pressing problems, many of which could be dealt with more effectively, some even solved to the extent that human problems can be solved, if only we could see the race question with more detachment, with less emotion (on both sides), and if we could keep it from obscuring problems with which it is not particularly concerned.

[28] Williams, *op. cit.*, chap. 3. Also V. O. Key, *Southern Politics in State and Nation* (New York: Knopf, 1949), pp. 6 ff.

[29] Key, *op. cit.*, p. 5.

I am not an uncritical admirer of the late Huey Long. His ruthless methods, his lack of plain honesty in office, his standards of behavior, were often intolerable. Our abhorrence of much that he did and stood for should not obscure either his achievement in building roads, bridges, and schools or the example he set in not introducing religion into politics and in not making a scapegoat of the Negro. He was not a fascist or a Nazi; he was, as Professor Williams says, an American boss.[30] He did not build political power on religious bigotry or race prejudice. With all his faults, and they were many, he kept before the voters the economic problems with which the state had to be concerned if it was to move out of a morass of poverty and ignorance. When he included Negroes in his welfare programs, he did so, not for idealistic reasons, but for solidly economic ones. He recognized what the lofty-minded abolitionists of the previous century failed to consider, that one large section or race of the South could not be permanently elevated unless other races and groups did not suffer in the process.

What of the contemporary political thought of the South? It is always difficult to stand aside and see the time in which one lives with the perspective possible to the view of a bygone day. Moreover, a comparison of the characteristics and the tendencies of the present time with those described by an acute observer, W. J. Cash in *The Mind of the South*,[31] written just before the Second World War, seems to lead to tentative observations, rather than to conclusions having the weight of certitude. In a little more than twenty years the changes appear in some respects very considerable, in others negligible. Any reasonably accurate generalization must be graduated, guarded by comparisons and contrasts between states and localities within states, between leaders of various categories—political, business, educational—even between segments of particular communities. The comments on the society, economic life, and politics of the South made by a group of careful scholars in 1948[32] offer many interesting and significant possibilities for comparison with those made a few years earlier by Cash, and those now found in scores of newspapers, magazines, scholarly journals, and books.

If I were to single out the one feature of political thought in the South of today which contrasts most vividly with that of the Old South of 1831–61, I would say that it is found in the wide range of opinion, the diversity of ideas and convictions. There are many indications of the survival of the rear-guard kind of negativism which dominated

[30] Williams, *op. cit.*, chap. 4.

[31] (New York: Knopf, 1941). See esp. secs. 21–24 of Book III, chap. 3.

[32] "The Southern Political Scene, 1938–1948," eds. Taylor Cole and John H. Hallowell, *Journal of Politics*, Vol. X, Nos. 2 and 3 (May and August, 1948).

Southern thinking and feeling in the two generations after 1830, but they are not in the majority in all states, or in any state at all times. The South is neither, as in the depression of the thirties, the nation's number one economic problem (some areas lead in prosperity) nor is it any longer accurately designated as the Solid South. The Solid South was, of course, never a one-party state in the sense in which Nazi Germany and Soviet Russia are one-party. But there has been a significant relaxing of narrow and unduly limiting standards of conformity in ideas regarding the South, the nation, the world.

It is encouraging that among the Southerners in office in Washington there is no placid uniformity of opinion. Who stands for the South, Senator Fulbright or Senator Byrd? Senator Yarborough or Senator Tower? Is the University of Mississippi or the University of North Carolina a more accurate representative of its educational future? So long as all are free to provide their answers to those and many other, and more involved, questions, the political and economic future of the South is in little danger of retreating into a sterile conformity which would, among other things, be false to its older and its finest traditions.

It is very easy to fall into the error of identifying the South with the century or so after 1830 and to ignore the two centuries and more before 1830. Thus Professor Clinton Rossiter, in his *Conservatism in America*,[33] remarks that "the South has always been the most conservative area in the United States." His explanation of that unqualified generalization is based largely upon the century after 1830, and upon the very recent reaction in parts of the South to the issue of desegregation, following the decision of the Supreme Court in 1954. He singles out such other examples of yearning for the old order of things as that oddity of the literary irreconcilables, the Nashville group's *I'll Take My Stand* (1930), a series of essays which reflects a longing for what was believed to have existed in the simple, slow-paced, agrarian Old South of a bygone day. It is a curious example of unhistorical nostalgia. But we can make allowances for the ignorance of history and economics displayed in graceful literary essays. A political scientist or a historian should take account of the *relative* rate of liberal change, even as regards the race problem, in most Southern cities, as compared with that in comparable areas of the North and West; there, too often, the movement has been in the direction of growing tension, rather than away from the folkways and the laws of the 1890's. And certainly one who deals with the conservative tradition in the United States should not commit himself to so sweeping a statement as that the South has "always" been the most conservative part of the country, a generalization which necessarily

[33] (Rev. ed.; New York: Vintage Books, 1962), pp. 227–32.

omits a large proportion of the achievements prior to 1828 or 1831. And even beyond that, for Andrew Jackson was also a Southerner.

It was in the South that the first representative assembly in America met. That was in Virginia in 1619. The same state adopted the first bill of rights and the first constitution intended to serve as a permanent instrument of government. That was in June, 1776, and the draftsman was the great plantation owner, George Mason. A few days later another Virginian wrote the Declaration of Independence. The motion for independence was introduced by Richard Henry Lee. A Southerner was both commander of the Continental Armies and president of the Federal Convention which produced the present Constitution. That document was more the work of another product of Virginia—James Madison—than of any other man, just as four of the first five Presidents and the greatest of our Chief Justices came from that state. Less spectacular, but essential, were the contributions of such men as Iredell and Davie from North Carolina, of Rutledge and the Pinckneys from South Carolina.

These men made permanent additions to the American tradition. Yet the usual stereotype of the Old South is that of the short and far from happy or successful thirty years before the War, and, as I have suggested, this ignores the contribution of Andrew Jackson. That period has been seen through rose-colored spectacles by so many novelists that even the historians deal with Southern history as though this short period was that of *the* Old South when, in simple fact, it was the last phase of the Old South. It was the era when, instead of providing leadership for the nation, as before 1831, the section let itself be placed in a purely defensive, isolated position from which there was no escape except by war, and that war was lost through no failure of its armies, but because the South was a minority, and a minority lacking the economic resources of the majority.

Not the least important cause of its comparative weakness was its failure to go along with the Industrial Revolution. Even Jefferson, who, during the Revolution, had expressed his fear of manufacturing and of cities, saw, early in the next century, that industrial development and a mixed economy were necessary for the country. Though he came to see the necessity of industrial diversification, he never altered his devotion to popular government, to tolerance, to the improvement of education. He remained convinced that slavery was morally and economically wrong and should be gradually abolished. Had the South followed his advice and remained true to his spirit, it would not have had the experience of poverty, of inferior education, of humiliation and defeat in a terribly costly war. The repudiation of Jefferson brought disaster.

That age is not, however, the age of Jefferson alone, for it was a time in which many farsighted men contributed their talents and their services.

Robert Lovett, born in Texas but known as a New York banker, in recent testimony before a Senate committee, reminds us of what was said by the philosopher Santayana: those who disregard the lessons of the past "are condemned to repeat it." My point is that the South has a choice of pasts, that there is a tradition older than the one too frequently accepted as that of the Old South, and that this tradition of the Older South of Washington, Jefferson, Madison, and Marshall, of Iredell, the Pinckneys, and Rutledge, of Jackson and many of his strongest supporters, is our rightful heritage, one of which we can be immensely proud, one which provides the spirit, though not necessarily the specific solutions, we should emulate.

Our circumstances are in many respects different from those of 1776 or 1787. Our needs are fundamentally the same. It is our good fortune that we do have a tradition which combines tolerance and a high standard of public service, freedom under law with orderly government, educational and economic advancement; that it is forward-looking, not dependent upon a legendary past which could not be recaptured even if it were in the interest of the South to do so. Those who would accept less for the South than the tradition which is its rightful heritage would be making a choice for which their descendants would not owe them the gratitude and the respect we have for the men of the South's greatest age.

ERNEST R. MAY

An American Tradition in Foreign Policy: The Role of Public Opinion

IN THE 1930's almost no article or speech on American foreign policy was complete without a reference to the three great traditions—no entangling alliances, the Monroe Doctrine, and the Open Door. By the end of the 1940's, all such references were out of date, or almost so. The United States had an alliance with its Latin-American neighbors, through the Rio treaty of 1948, and one with the free nations of Europe through the North Atlantic Treaty; the Monroe Doctrine had been replaced, at least in part, by pledges of co-operative action with the American republics; the Open Door had been shut by the Chinese Communists.

Nowadays, anyone attempting to deal with traditions in American foreign policy faces two choices. He may stretch the term to fit policies developed since World War II and discuss such topics as "the tradition of containment" and "the tradition of deterrence." (I am reminded of a placard I once saw offering tickets to a student organization's "First Traditional Midwinter Ball.") Alternatively, he may hypothesize abstract traditions of which people were not conscious at the time. This is not unrewarding; something of the sort is a central occupation of political scientists who write of realism and idealism in American ideology. I prefer, however, to take neither course but to set aside questions concerning traditions *in* American policy and explore a tradition *about* American policy.

This tradition is that which the Soviet scholar Y. Osokin derides in the January, 1962, issue of the Moscow journal *International Affairs.* He writes:

ERNEST R. MAY is Professor of History at Harvard University. In 1963–64, after this essay was originally prepared, the author had the good fortune to be a fellow of the Center for Advanced Study in the Behavioral Sciences, and he is deeply indebted to the Center and the community of fellows for help in revising and improving it.

Independent public opinion is one of the favourite fetishes invented by the ideologists of the capitalist system in general and the "American way of life" in particular. Without any grounds whatsoever this "opinion" is claimed to have real supreme sovereignty. . . . It is a kind of "categoric imperative" for Governments which merely have to carry out the dictates of "public opinion."

Speaking of *The Policy Machine: The Department of State and American Foreign Policy* by Professor Robert Ellsworth Elder, Osokin makes free with the book's data and goes on to assert:

It is not public opinion that influences the State Department but on the contrary the State Department manufactures public opinion with the help of an apparatus expressly created for this purpose.

To begin with, the State Department controls the so-called "independent press" by means of briefing daily the correspondents of the 25 biggest newspapers and news agencies. . . .

More than that. The State Department also has a well organized apparatus for the direct conditioning of public opinion, the so-called Office of Public Services. . . .

The Staff workers of the office read over 1,000 lectures throughout the country every year. Its propaganda materials . . . are distributed in millions of copies. This is a colossal "kitchen" in which the State Department "prepares public opinion," so often falsely described in American propaganda as the decisive factor in the country's foreign policy.

Almost any American reading these words must feel that Osokin either doesn't know the truth about the United States or that he is distorting it to fit a party line. We would respond thus, because what he is challenging is one of our most powerful traditions: our faith that public policy is an expression of public opinion, and our corollary faith that public opinion is opinion originating among the public not opinion forced or foisted on the people by the government.

But is it enough of an answer to Osokin and similar critics merely to restate this tradition? Do we in fact *know* that it is well-founded or do we merely assume so? Looking at American historical writing, one would find apparent confirmation of the tradition. With a few noteworthy exceptions, historians of European international relations have concentrated on exchanges between diplomats or, as G. M. Young has said somewhat unfairly, on what one clerk said to another clerk; few have studied public opinion.[1] Historians of United States foreign rela-

---

[1] Among the exceptions are the pioneer English works, George Carslake Thompson, *Public Opinion and Lord Beaconsfield, 1875–1880* (London, 1886), and A. V. Dicey, *Lectures on the Relation of Law and Public Opinion in England during the Nineteenth Century* (London, 1914); Eckart Kehr's model interest group study, *Schlachtflottenbau- und Parteipolitik* (Berlin, 1930); and some books by American scholars, notably E. M. Carroll, *French Public Opinion and Foreign Affairs, 1870–1914* (New York, 1931), and *Germany and the Great Powers, 1866–1914: A Study in Public Opinion and Foreign Policy* (New York, 1938); Lynn M. Case, *French*

tions, on the other hand, have written more about public opinion than about diplomacy. A leading textbook, that by Thomas A. Bailey, is entitled *A Diplomatic History of the American People*, and standard works on such topics as the War of 1812, the Mexican War, the war of 1898, and the isolationism of the 1920's and 1930's focus on public attitudes. Even books that center on diplomacy at least pay lip service to the importance of public opinion. Critics of the American ideology, such as Hans Morgenthau and George Kennan, start with the assumption that governmental views reflect public views; what they say, at least implicitly, is that this should not be so—that policies should come to a larger extent from calculations by experts.

However, one may legitimately ask whether these historical studies demonstrate the validity of the tradition or merely demonstrate that American historians have taken its validity for granted. In recent years, increasing numbers of social scientists have given attention to individual opinions, the ways in which public opinion is formed, and the means by which opinions are communicated. Some of their findings cast doubt on our common assumptions. Indeed, these findings pose the question of whether our traditional interpretation of the relation between public opinion and foreign policy is not largely mythical.

To begin with, there are suggestive studies by psychologists about the nature of individual opinions. Some of these studies indicate that people may develop opinions on public issues because doing so helps them privately—to release subconscious aggressions or meet problems of social adjustment or gratify quite irrelevant desires.

Some years ago there was published a now-famous study on "the authoritarian personality." It contended that common elements could be found in the psychological makeup of people who held strong racial prejudices. Most of them, said the authors, had similar patterns of social and sexual behavior and evidenced similar suppressed emotions and impulses toward submissiveness. While the methodology of the researchers has been questioned, their scale of personality measurement has proved a useful tool. Significant correlations have been found between authoritarianism and opposition to the United Nations, support for the strategic views of General Douglas MacArthur, jingoism, and expectation of war. Similarly, correlations have been found between low authoritarianism and internationalism or "worldmindedness."[2]

Opinion on War and Diplomacy during the Second Empire (Philadelphia, 1954); and Arno Mayer's ideological analysis, *The Political Origins of the New Diplomacy* (New Haven, 1959).

[2] T. W. Adorno, Else Frenkel Brunswick, D. J. Levinson, and R. N. Sanford, *The Authoritarian Personality* (New York, 1950). Criticisms include Richard Christie and Marie Jahoda (eds.), *Studies in the Scope and Method of "The Authoritarian Personality"* (Glencoe,

One study in depth made by a team of psychologists at Harvard involved intensive interviews and tests of ten men from varying backgrounds and occupations over a two-year period just after World War II.[3] The study sought to establish the relationships, if any, between the personalities and the attitudes of these men toward the Soviet Union, which was just then ceasing to be an ally and becoming an enemy. One of the ten was found to be very sympathetic toward Russia, critical of the American press for its treatment of the Soviets, and critical of American failure to be more trustful and co-operative. In his childhood, this man had idealized his father, a sickly workman often down on his luck; he had been antagonistic toward his mother, who ruled the family sternly and continually berated the father. His own life had had ups and downs; he had been continually seeking security yet rejecting it whenever it came—in marriage or in opportunities for steady employment. He had developed a compulsive need to be eccentric or different in order to draw attention to himself. The psychologists surmised that his idealization of Russia had some relation to his feelings for his father, that his attitude toward the press was related to his feelings toward his mother, that communism was identified in his mind with security and therefore attracted him, and that he got pleasure from shocking his acquaintances by standing up for a nation they were beginning to distrust.

The other of the ten who was most antagonistic toward Russia was

---

Ill., 1954); Angus Campbell, Philip E. Converse, Warren E. Miller, and Donald E. Stokes, *The American Voter* (New York, 1960), pp. 512–15; and, most devastating of all, Gerhard E. Lenski and John C. Leggett, "Caste, Class, and Deference in the Research Interview," *American Journal of Sociology*, LXV (March, 1960), 463–67. The original study showed that interviewees from the lower socio-economic rungs expressed frequent agreement with propositions indicative of authoritarianism. Lenski and Leggett found that, if the propositions were reversed, interviewees from these groups would still express agreement. This suggests that a working stiff being questioned by a young college girl is predisposed to say, "Yes'm." Nevertheless, see H. Edwin Titus and E. P. Hollander, "The California F. Scale in Psychological Research, 1950–1955," *Psychological Bulletin*, LIV (January, 1957), 47–64; Morris Janowitz and Dwaine Marvick, "Authoritarianism and Political Behavior," *Public Opinion Quarterly*, XVII (Summer, 1955), 185–201; Robert E. Lane, "Political Personality and Electoral Choice," *American Political Science Review*, XLIX (March, 1955), 173–90; Daniel J. Levinson, "Authoritarian Personality and Foreign Policy," *Journal of Conflict Resolution*, I (March, 1957), 37–47; Howard P. Smith and Ellen W. Rosen, "Some Psychological Correlates of Worldmindedness and Authoritarianism," *Journal of Personality*, XXVI (June, 1958), 170–83; and Bjørn Christiansen, *Attitudes toward Foreign Affairs as a Function of Personality* (Oslo, 1959). Charles D. Farris, "Selected Attitudes on Foreign Affairs as Correlates of Authoritarianism and Political Anomie," *Journal of Politics*, XXII (February, 1960), 50–67, reports a further correlation between hypernationalism and a sense of alienation or political ineffectuality. Maurice Farber, "Psychoanalytic Hypotheses in the Study of War," *Journal of Social Issues*, I (1955), 29–35, goes on to argue a correlation with anality. See also Irving Sarnoff, "Psychoanalytic Theory and Social Attitudes," *Public Opinion Quarterly*, XXIV (Summer, 1960), 251–79.

[3] M. Brewster Smith, Jerome S. Bruner, and Robert H. White, *Opinions and Personality* (New York, 1956).

a small businessman born into a white-collar family on the social skids who was forced to make his own way up from a common laborer to a respectability similar to that which his parents had lost. Testers commented of him: "His admiration for courage, physical strength, and the taking of strong stands [are] compensations for an early timidity and sense of physical inferiority, compensations . . . doing some service of inner reassurance." All ten cases pointed to the conclusion that an individual's opinion on a foreign policy issue might be less a considered response to events or situations than a reflection of his own character, personality, or temperament.

In and by itself, this conclusion would neither shatter the traditional idea that foreign policy mirrors public opinion nor invalidate the historical reconstructions reinforcing that tradition. Hardly anyone is so doctrinaire as to say that the public's judgments are always reasonable. Even in Lincoln's famous apothegm, it is conceded that all of the people can be fooled some of the time and some of the people all of the time. Almost every historian has treated one group or another as if it were irrational. Proponents of war and opponents of international co-operation have often been so characterized, and some of the more recent writings on the jingoism of 1898 and the isolationism of 1919–39 are actually psychopathological in approach.[4] The findings of psychologists do, however, raise unsettling questions.

First of all, they stimulate relativistic speculation, causing one to wonder anew how any opinions can be judged more reasonable than others. In the thirties, when historians looked back to 1914–17, they were at a loss to explain as other than pathological the drives of those Americans who advocated intervention in the European war. Historians looking back from the sixties find the interventionists relatively easy to understand. From their standpoint, it is the historians of the thirties who seem queer.[5] Perhaps one can infer that images of the past are determined not only by the rational biases of historians but by personality traits shared by those who are drawn to the writing of history. This would suggest that truth in history is wholly beyond recapture.

Fortunately, these psychological studies are offset by others. It may well be true, as Sidney Verba contends, that the more importance a public issue has for an individual, the more likely it is that his opinion on that issue will be a function of his personality and an expression of

---

[4] See Richard Hofstadter, "Manifest Destiny and the Philippines," in Daniel Aaron (ed.), *America in Crisis* (New York, 1952); Ernest R. May, *Imperial Democracy: The Emergence of America as a Great Power* (New York, 1961); Selig Adler, *The Isolationist Impulse* (New York, 1957); and Robert A. Divine, *The Illusion of Neutrality* (Chicago, 1962).

[5] See Ernest R. May, *Intervention, 1917 and 1941*, American Historical Association Pamphlet, 1959.

deep-seated drives.[6] On the other hand, a considerable body of data shows that a man's mind makes adjustments to bring one attitude or opinion into congruence with others, and studies in test situations demonstrate that individuals can change their attitudes and opinions as they acquire new information or new perspectives.[7] For what it is worth, there is also evidence that opinions vary with education. Samuel Stouffer made a nationwide survey in 1954 of opinions on communism, civil liberties, and McCarthyism. After much questioning, interviewing, and tabulating, he found that variations corresponded more with educational level than with any other factor. The less educated the interviewee, the more worried he was about the menace of Communist subversion, and the more he approved such methods as McCarthy's. The better educated he was, the more he saw Communists in the United States as presenting little danger and McCarthy's methods as reprehensible and immoral.[8]

While these data suggest at least that some opinions are more firmly grounded than others, they do not, unhappily, suggest criteria that can be applied either to the past or the present. If an American historian were to assume that the better-educated part of the population had always been the more reasonable part, he would find himself, in effect, siding with the Tories, the Federalists, the social Darwinists, and those who held (with F. D. R.'s budget director) that failure to maintain the gold standard would mean the ruin of Western civilization. The absence of objective criteria for judgment is not, of course, a new problem for historians. They have long been torn between the impulse to be hanging judges, as Lord Acton advises, or, as Sir Herbert Butterfield admonishes, to be "technical historians," appraising in terms of results (and thus running the risk, as A. J. P. Taylor argues, of saying that Hitler killed six million Jews and did an excellent job according to his lights).[9] As yet, the findings of psychologists do not suggest an escape from this age-old dilemma.

Evidence as to the role of personality in opinion formation also provokes another question. This has to do with the judgment of public opinion by the men who act for the public. Studies on the effectiveness of communications have confirmed a hypothesis advanced by Pierce, James, and Dewey. The human mind does filter what is heard and seen,

[6] Sidney Verba, "Assumptions of Rationality and Non-Rationality in Models of the International System," *World Politics*, XIV (October, 1961), 92–117.

[7] See Carl I. Hovland, Irving L. Janis, and Harold H. Kelley, *Communications and Persuasion* (New Haven, 1953); Harold H. Kelley and John W. Thibaut, "Experimental Studies of Group Problem Solving and Process," in Gardner Lindzey (ed.), *Handbook of Social Psychology* (2 vols.; Cambridge, Mass., 1954), II, 735–85; and the special issue of the *Public Opinion Quarterly*, XXIV (Summer, 1960), devoted to attitude change.

[8] Samuel A. Stouffer, *Communism, Conformity, and Civil Liberties* (New York, 1955).

[9] A. J. P. Taylor, *Rumours of Wars* (London, 1952), p. 11.

selecting for notice or retention primarily those data that are relevant to its concerns. In addition, the mind apparently tends to reject or ignore data that would jar opinions or beliefs that are functions of the personality.[10] The processes are extremely complex, and experimentation has happily not upset all common-sense suppositions. Not only can information and argumentation change opinions, but external reality has something to do with shaping them, and the more intelligent a man is, the more responsive he is to logical argument (provided that he is comparatively well-adjusted psychologically).[11] Nevertheless, one is left with the question as to whether statesmen, in appraising public opinion, may not be arriving at judgments that are products of their own personalities and inner needs.

Awareness of the irrational has, of course, been with us for a long time. Freudian concepts have often been used in political analysis, but usually in connection with such relatively obvious subjects as Naziism. Their implications with regard to American democracy have been explored only cursorily. Even from the few studies mentioned here, it is clear, however, that many of the propositions running through political and historical writing are, to say the least, questionable. In such writing one finds it said, for example, that the public in 1920 pined for normalcy, that the bulk of the people in the 1930's was isolationist, and that the public by 1952 was weary of the Korean War. Each such statement implies the existence of widely shared values and criteria leading to common judgments. Each presupposes that politicians, journalists, political scientists, and historians can infer these values, criteria, and judgments from the scraps of evidence they collect. Psychological research

[10] Martin Scheerer, "Cognitive Theory," in Lindzey, *Handbook of Social Psychology*, I, 91–142; Bernard Berelson, Paul F. Lazarsfeld, and William McPhee, *Voting* (Chicago, 1954), pp. 277–304; Leon Festinger, *A Theory of Cognitive Dissonance* (Evanston, Ill., 1957); Joseph T. Klapper, "What We Know about the Effects of Mass Communication: The Brink of Hope," *Public Opinion Quarterly*, XXI (Winter, 1957–58), 453–74; Fritz Heider, *The Psychology of Interpersonal Relations* (New York, 1958); W. Philips Davison, "On the Effects of Communication," *Public Opinion Quarterly*, XXIII (Fall, 1959), 343–60; C. E. Osgood, "Cognitive Dissonance in the Conduct of Human Affairs," *ibid.*, XXIV (Summer, 1960), 341–65; R. B. Zajonc, "The Concepts of Balance, Congruity, and Dissonance," *ibid.*, pp. 280–96; Nathan Maccoby and Eleanor E. Maccoby, "Homeostatic Theory in Attitude Change," *ibid.*, XXV (Winter, 1961), 538–45; Joseph T. Klapper, "Mass Communications Research: An Old Road Resurveyed," *ibid.*, XXVII (Winter, 1963), 515–27.

[11] Hovland, Janis, and Kelley, *Communications and Persuasion*, pp. 181–204; Morris Rosenberg and Paul F. Lazarsfeld (eds.), *The Language of Social Research* (Glencoe, Ill., 1955), pp. 392–93; Carl I. Hovland and Irving L. Janis, *Personality and Persuasibility* (New Haven, 1959); Milton J. Rosenberg, Carl I. Hovland, William J. McGuire, Robert P. Abelson, and Jack W. Brehan, *Attitude Organization and Change: An Analysis of Consistency among Attitude Components* (New Haven, 1960); Muzafer Sherif and Carl I. Hovland, *Social Judgment: Assimilation and Contrast Effects in Communication and Attitude Change* (New Haven, 1961); Herbert C. Kelman, "Processes of Opinion Change," *Public Opinion Quarterly*, XXV (Spring, 1961), 57–78.

voices a warning that individual systems of rationality differ widely, that what one man regards as reasonable another may regard as lunatic, that a great deal of information is necessary to understand just the opinions of one person, let alone those of a multitude, and that interpretations of public opinion depend to some extent on the system of rationality peculiar to the interpreter.

While research on individual opinions does not itself support a thesis such as Osokin's, it does provide an argument by which governmental manipulation of public opinion might be justified. Research that has been done on opinion formation within groups has more direct relevance to the question of whether or not his thesis is supportable.

Some of this research has also been done by psychologists. One common-sense assumption that they have substantiated is that individuals arrive at opinions in part through identification with groups. People want to hold views that conform or at least are not at sharp variance with those of other people to whom they look for approval. The group may be a "primary group," the circle of family and friends, or it may be a wider "reference group." A man may conceive of himself, for example, as belonging to the upper class or the "better element," and he may be influenced to adopt certain opinions or attitudes because he thinks them appropriate to that class. Status, occupation, ethnic origin, religion, locale, residence, or any number of other factors can be the basis for such a group identification. In some instances, the point of reference may be another individual, either real or idealized: "a reference idol." William James pointed out long ago that even an apparent nonconformist may look for some such external support. The "social self" seeks to prove itself "at least *worthy* of approving recognition by the highest possible judging companion."[12] But where the group is actual and the members seek some kind of consensus, the individual opinions begin to become collective and thus potentially "public."

Little research has gone into the question of how individuals choose reference groups or reference idols. One is left to infer that the processes are part and parcel of those that produce opinions themselves. In other words, they are deeply rooted in individual personalities. Young men may, for example, identify with groups to which their families belong or they may equally well reject these identifications, depending in part on what their relationships with their families have been. There are many varying systems of rationality, and political and historical writing seems in error in presupposing identity of opinion among groups that

[12] William James, *Principles of Psychology* (2 vols.; New York, 1890), I, 316. See Herbert H. Hyman, "Reflections on Reference Groups," *Public Opinion Quarterly*, XXIV (Fall, 1960), 383–96.

have externally observable characteristics in common. It should be said, however, that historical writing is sometimes more sophisticated than current political commentary. Most journalists and political scientists talk of businessmen, Roman Catholics, Mexican-Americans, and comparable groups as units. Historians have learned, at least in some instances, not to use such categories. They no longer make such assertions as that bondholders supported ratification of the Constitution, that businessmen opposed the progressive movement, or that Midwesterners, German-Americans, and Irish-Americans were isolationist.[13] Differences exist, it is true, only in instances where there has been intensive historical research. Elsewhere historians resort to the same generalizations as journalists and political scientists. But historical research does complement psychological research in suggesting that the concept of the group is not itself the key that will enable social scientists to make assertions about public opinion that they cannot make about individual opinions.

Research by sociologists and political scientists has developed much data about how opinions circulate within groups, no matter how these group opinions develop. In 1944, Paul Lazarsfeld and Bernard Berelson published a study of voting behavior in Erie County, Ohio, during the 1940 presidential election. This book, now regarded as a classic in the relatively new field of survey research, was based on intensive and repeated interviews with a carefully selected sample. One of the findings was that personal influence had been a key factor in determining vote changes. In general, people had paid more heed to people they knew than to speeches by candidates, news reported through the mass media, or campaign work by party organizations. The study identified a certain proportion of the population as "opinion leaders": people to whom others turned for information or advice.[14]

[13] Charles A. Beard, *An Economic Interpretation of the Constitution* (New York, 1913), is taken apart in Forrest McDonald, *We the People: The Economic Origins of the Constitution* (Chicago, 1958), and Robert E. Brown, *Charles Beard and the Constitution* (Princeton, 1956). See also Lee Benson, *Turner and Beard, American Historical Writing Reconsidered* (Glencoe, Ill., 1960), pp. 95–213. On businessmen and Progressivism see R. H. Wiebe, *Businessmen and Reform* (Cambridge, Mass., 1962). George L. Grassmuck, *Sectional Biases in Congress on Foreign Policy* (Baltimore, 1951), and Ralph H. Smuckler, "The Region of Isolationism," *American Political Science Review*, XLVII (Sept. 1953), 386–401, are examples of geographical interpretation; Samuel Lubell, *The Future of American Politics* (New York, 1956), and Adler, *The Isolationist Impulse*, lean toward the ethnic-origin interpretation; LeRoy N. Rieselbach, "The Basis of Isolationist Behavior," *Public Opinion Quarterly*, XXIV (Winter, 1960), 645–57, and Bruce M. Russett, "Demography, Salience, and Isolationist Behavior," *ibid.*, pp. 658–64, supply evidence that self-identification with conservatism and Republicanism and degree of interest in foreign affairs may have been more important than either locale or ethnic origin.

[14] Paul F. Lazarsfeld, Bernard Berelson, and Hazel Gaudet, *The People's Choice* (New York, 1944).

Making a similar study in Elmira, New York, during the 1948 election, Lazarsfeld and Berelson found confirmation of this hypothesis. In Erie County, they had been surprised to learn of the role of personal influence. This time they made a point of studying it more closely. The more they saw of it, the more complicated it seemed. They write:

> For leadership in political discussion people mainly turn to others like themselves. The banker and mayor and union officer may be "opinion leaders" in a distant sense, but ordinary voters listen to near-by influencers. For this reason, one might properly speak less of leaders than of a complex web of opinion-leading relationships. It is true that one can single out those individuals who are more likely than others to be at the center of several such relationships and call them "opinion leaders." . . . But when it is found also that the people so singled out as leaders report, in turn, that they *seek advice* on politics more than others . . . we are reminded again that in practice there must be unending circuits of leadership relationships running through the community, like a nerve system through the body.[15]

Lazarsfeld and Elihu Katz subsequently made a study of women in Decatur, Illinois, seeking to determine what role personal influence played in decisions other than political. They found that most people decided which products to buy on the basis not of advertisements but of word-of-mouth advice. The voting studies had hypothesized a "two-step flow of communications." Information and argument in the mass media, it appeared, did not reach the masses directly but reached opinion leaders, were absorbed by them, and then passed on by them. In Decatur, Lazarsfeld and Katz found this same pattern operating. They also discerned, however, that there was more than one web of leadership in the community. Examining the development of opinions on public issues, they found that certain comparatively well-educated women occupied key points in the circuits. On the other hand, when the subject was brands of groceries, these key points were occupied by mothers of large families. When it was clothing styles or movies, the points were held by young unmarried women. "Any image of the process of interpersonal relations," they concluded, "must now be revised to include *horizontal* opinion leadership, that is, leadership which emerges on each rung of the socio-economic ladder, and all through the community."[16]

Studies by other scholars suggest similar conclusions. Beginning with the Lynds' celebrated analyses of "Middletown" (Muncie, Indiana), community studies have reported the existence of opinion leaders. One by Robert K. Merton distinguished two groups, one of which led opinion

[15] Berelson, Lazarsfeld, and McPhee, *Voting*, pp. 109–10.

[16] Elihu Katz and Paul F. Lazarsfeld, *Personal Influence: The Part Played by People in the Flow of Mass Communications* (Glencoe, Ill., 1955), p. 325. See also Elihu Katz, "The Two-Step Flow of Communications: An Up-To-Date Report on an Hypothesis," *Public Opinion Quarterly*, XXI (Spring, 1957), 61–78.

on town, the other on national, affairs. Merton termed these respectively "locals" and "cosmopolitans," and he was able to distinguish between them in terms of occupation and even reading habits.[17] A survey of "locals" in a small town revealed the existence of a communications network. Opinions on civic issues were generated within a relatively small group of men who were comparatively prosperous and high in social status. Others in the town, generally less well-off and less well-read, asked their opinions and then spread them around, either borrowing outright or saying candidly, "So-and-so says such-and-such." A larger number of the town's population thus heard the views of the community leaders. When polled, most gave the opinions of these leaders as their own. A survey in a Midwestern suburb, seeking to determine how views developed on foreign policy issues, found a similar network radiating out from "cosmopolitans."[18]

To a large extent, these findings represent a rediscovery rather than a discovery. They confirm an assumption that some scholars had made earlier. Writing on American public opinion in the late nineteenth century, Lord Bryce had hypothesized the existence of an opinion-forming elite. One of the founders of American sociology, Edward A. Ross, wrote in 1908: "Every editor, politician, banker, capitalist, railroad president, employer, clergyman, or judge has a following with whom his opinion has weight. He, in turn, is likely to have *his* authorities. The anatomy of collective opinion shows it to be organized from centers and subcenters, forming a kind of intellectual feudal system."[19] Nevertheless, the working of personal influence and the existence of opinion leadership in each locality are important facts which commentary on American policy and American traditions has all too often ignored.

Some social scientists have speculated about the existence of a national elite from which opinions on foreign policy filter down to "cosmopolitans" in each community. In a pioneer synthesis, Gabriel Almond suggested that such a group might be composed of high government officials, civil servants expert on foreign policy issues, leaders in organizations

---

[17] Robert K. Merton, "Patterns of Influence: A Study of Interpersonal Influence and Communications Behavior in a Local Community," in Paul F. Lazarsfeld and Frank Stanton (eds.), *Communications Research, 1948–49* (New York, 1949). See Robert S. and Helen M. Lynd, *Middletown* (New York, 1929), pp. 478–95, and *Middletown in Transition* (New York, 1937), pp. 74–101 and 319–72; W. Lloyd Warner and Paul S. Lunt, *The Social Life of a Modern Community* (New Haven, 1941); Floyd Hunter, *Community Power Structure* (Chapel Hill, 1953); and Robert A. Dahl, *Who Governs? Democracy and Power in an American City* (New Haven, 1961).

[18] Robert E. Agger and Vincent Ostrom, "The Political Structure of a Small Community," *Public Opinion Quarterly*, XX (Spring, 1956), 81–89; Kenneth P. Adler and Davis Bobrow, "Interest and Influence in Foreign Affairs," *ibid.*, pp. 89–101.

[19] James Bryce, *The American Commonwealth* (2 vols., New York, 1888), II, 209–334; E. A. Ross, *Social Psychology* (New York, 1908), p. 348.

with direct or abstract interest in such issues, and journalists in all the various mass media. Others have gone so far as to argue the existence of a tightly-knit, almost conspiratorial "Establishment" practically dictating public opinion on crucial issues. Writing facetiously, Richard Rovere of *The New Yorker* describes the Council on Foreign Relations as its board of directors and the *New York Times* as its official organ.[20] From sociological data, some American scholars and journalists have thus approached a conclusion very similar to that of the Russian Osokin.

As yet, this conclusion has neither been proven nor widely accepted. With careful reasoning—which parallels that of other political scientists dealing with domestic affairs—Almond argues that to affirm the existence of opinion-forming elites is neither to deny that the United States is a democracy nor to say that the attitudes and moods of the masses are inconsequential. In several senses, members of these elites are representatives or delegates; the people who pay attention to them are their constituents, with whom, like elected representatives, they have to remain in tune; and, as Almond writes, their very position as trusted experts "involves a constant search for the most adequate means to realize the values of their clienteles. . . ."[21]

Like the findings of psychologists, nevertheless, these findings by sociologists jar the conception of democracy that we carry over almost unchanged from the age of the Enlightenment. The traditional model of democracy is that of the courtroom. The advocates for differing points of view are the lawyers. They stand before the vast jury that is the public, and the members of that jury hear them, weigh their arguments, and then arrive at considered verdicts. But, the researches of both psychologists and sociologists indicate that the processes are much more intricate and much less rational—at least in the sense of conforming to a single system of rationality—that this traditional concept assumes. This evidence seems to lend plausibility rather than the reverse to such an attack as Osokin's. If issues are actually judged not in terms of intrinsic merits but by standards that are peculiar to each individual, and if judgment is in fact guided by opinion-forming elites, then it is not inconceivable that in certain circumstances government officials could create and manipulate the public opinion that, in theory, they were obeying.

[20] Gabriel A. Almond, *The American People and Foreign Policy* (New York, 1950), pp. 139–41; C. Wright Mills, *The Power Elite* (New York, 1956); Floyd Hunter, *Top Leadership, U.S.A.* (Chapel Hill, 1959); Richard Rovere, "Notes on the Establishment in America," *American Scholar*, XXX (Autumn, 1961), 489–95.

[21] Almond, *The American People and Foreign Policy*, p. 237. See also V. O. Key, Jr., *Politics, Parties, and Pressure Groups* (2d ed.; New York, 1948), pp. 178–84; David B. Truman, *The Governmental Process: Political Interests and Public Opinion* (New York, 1951); and Robert A. Dahl, *A Preface to Democratic Theory* (Chicago, 1956).

It should be said immediately that the researches of social scientists do not demonstrate such a proposition. In fact, it is precisely at this crucial point that their studies run thin. Few have investigated the actual connections between public opinion and policy.

Some work has been done on such questions as how public opinion is transmitted to and received by men who make policy and how these men respond to what they apprehend as public opinion. When asked by one researcher how they learned of public feeling, a number of Congressmen gave as their primary source letters from their constituents, and conversations with callers and visits to their home districts as the next best source, but they rated public opinion polls as generally of little utility. Officials in the executive branch apparently accord the polls more respect. Some departments even conduct their own private polls. But the officials who admit to attaching considerable weight to these samplings are men of relatively low rank. What the situation is at higher levels, no one quite knows. While poll results reach the desk of the President, so do careful summaries of trends in the mail. Some past Presidents have regularly read random samples of letters addressed to them and have regarded these as a major index to public sentiment.[22] It seems to be the case that among all officials who keep an eye on the electorate the contents of the mailbag receive more attention than do straw votes or polls.

In a study of the press and foreign policy, Bernard C. Cohen declares that most officials in the State Department use newspapers as their "*daily* measure of how people are reacting to the ebb and flow of . . . developments. . . . In fact," he adds, "many officials treat the press and public opinion as synonymous."[23] But Congressmen apparently pay less attention to the press. At any rate, Cohen describes a forthcoming work which will report that, on foreign policy issues, there is almost no correlation between legislators' stands and the editorial stands of papers in their districts.[24] And it is not at all clear that the attitude of State Department officials toward the press is shared in the White House. Democratic Presidents from Wilson through Johnson have all spoken of the press, which is largely Republican, as unrepresentative. The case most often mentioned in which presidential policy is supposed to have

[22] Martin Kriesberg, "What Congressmen Think of the Polls," *Public Opinion Quarterly*, IX (Fall, 1945), 333–37; Truman, *The Governmental Process*, pp. 389–91; Bernard C. Cohen, *The Political Process and Foreign Policy: The Making of the Japanese Peace Settlement* (Princeton, 1957), pp. 210–15. See also the comments by two public officials (Adam Yarmolinsky and Launor F. Carter) and one public opinion researcher (Ithiel de Sola Pool) in *Public Opinion Quarterly*, XXVII (Winter, 1963), 543–61.

[23] Bernard C. Cohen, *The Press and Foreign Policy* (Princeton, 1963), p. 234.

[24] Warren E. Miller and Donald E. Stokes, "Representation in Congress," cited *ibid.*, p. 240.

been changed by press reaction is that of Roosevelt's 1937 Quarantine speech. The President told a Chicago audience that the 90 per cent of nations who loved peace should quarantine the 10 per cent who were aggressive. A few days afterward, he repudiated the notion that he had been suggesting collective sanctions and said, in effect, that his figure of speech had been meaningless. The common assumption has been that his retreat was due to adverse editorial reaction. But this has been disproved. Dorothy Borg has demonstrated that initial press comment was unexpectedly favorable. If Roosevelt backed down because he feared that the public would not support him (which is what most of his associates thought), it was because he had seen signs of this elsewhere, perhaps in the mail or in conversations with visitors. What the episode may demonstrate is that Roosevelt did *not* regard press comment as reflective of public opinion.[25] We simply do not know the extent to which, in the White House, newspapers are regarded as mirrors of opinion.

If we know little about the sources in which officials read public opinion, we know even less about what they look for in these sources. If it is true that Congressmen and Presidents pay more heed to mail than to other indices, that fact, at first glance, is surprising. Pollsters are now quite sophisticated in selecting representative samples and in asking meaningful questions. In spite of their miscalculation in 1948, they have been remarkably accurate in predicting elections, and one might think that men in public life would regard poll results as far more reliable indices of public opinion than letters or chance conversations.

But there is one reasonable hypothesis that would explain why mail in particular is accorded such weight. It is that public officials are less interested in the kinds of information that polls yield than in the kinds of information that can sometimes be extracted from letters. Quite often, they may be concerned not with how the public reacts to what has been done but rather with how it may react to some step that is contemplated. Although political scientists have given considerable attention to "latent" public opinion, no one has devised methods for gauging it, and it seems unlikely that such methods can be devised.[26] It may be that letters or conversations give an experienced man the best hints that he can get as to what latent opinion may be.

In addition, it is possible that public officials are primarily concerned with intensities and nuances in opinion rather than with mere quantities. There are polling techniques designed to distinguish those who hold a

[25] Dorothy Borg, "Notes on Roosevelt's 'Quarantine' Speech," *Political Science Quarterly*, LXXII (Sept., 1957), 405–33.

[26] See V. O. Key, Jr., *Public Opinion and American Democracy* (New York, 1961), pp. 263–87.

view strongly from those who merely incline toward it. But these are crude distinctions in comparison with those that can be made by analyzing carefully an individual's opinions. Working for a prolonged period with a handful of subjects, the Harvard psychologists who studied attitudes toward the Soviet Union were able to discriminate among such attributes as informational support, differentiation, time perspective, and saliency.[27]

Each of these terms probably requires a word of explanation. Informational support, while its meaning is obvious, implies something about the strength and stability of an opinion. For example, one would not expect an individual's view about the Oppenheimer case to be hard and fast if he were one of those who, when asked by a pollster to define "nuclear physicist," responded, "He's a spy," "Something to do with New Dealers," or "Studies eggs, doesn't he?"[28]

Differentiation has to do with the terms in which individuals see issues. Writing of reactions to the Army-McCarthy hearings, Gerhart Wiebe observes, "Some 45 per cent . . . perceived the hearings as a contest between decent men and a ruffian . . . [and] cheered for the decent men. Another group, in the neighborhood of 33 per cent, saw the issue as a contest between sob sisters and a righteous crusader, and they rooted for righteousness."[29] Whether one sees an issue as moral or practical, economic or political, national or local (to suggest other terms of reference), affects the intensity of an opinion.

Time perspective is something else. Before the limited test-ban treaty of 1963, there were proponents of a ban who regarded it as urgent, others who felt that it would become urgent within a few years, and still others who held that a ban, while desirable, could be delayed for an indefinite period. These opinions, while similar, varied in intensity.

Saliency has to do with the relative importance to the individual of a given issue. A mother whose child had already had a maximum dosage of X-rays probably viewed the test ban issue somewhat differently from an equally ardent opponent of testing whose interest was just in the public weal. For the former, the question had greater saliency.

While these terms are not ones that politicians would ordinarily use, the distinctions are ones to which politicians presumably are sensitive. Experienced public men declare that they can tell a form letter almost at a glance. Those letters that are not forms they know to have been written by people who really care about the issue. In or between the lines they may be able to read much else. Perhaps officeholders pay more

[27] Smith, Bruner, and White, *Opinions and Personality*, pp. 33–37.

[28] *Public Opinion Quarterly*, XI (Winter, 1947–48), 661.

[29] G. D. Wiebe, "The Army-McCarthy Hearings and the Public Conscience," *ibid.*, XXII (Winter, 1958–59), 490–502.

attention to mail than to polls because even the best polls cannot tell them as much about how well the interested citizenry understands an issue, in what context it is viewed, and how important it may be to particular individuals.

One additional reason might be recognition by officeholders that the mail puts them in touch with opinion leaders. Researchers who have identified such leaders have found that they lay great stress on writing letters to Washington. One who interviewed businessmen to learn what pressures, if any, had been applied for or against reciprocal trade legislation reported his unexpected finding that most "regarded *writing* Congressmen as the basic political-legislative act. . . . [N]early all of them said, 'I wrote,' 'I telegraphed,' or 'No, I haven't written,' when asked if they had done something about the issue."[30]

Two studies giving attention to governmental sources of information on public opinion suggest that the legislative and executive branches hear from different kinds of opinion leaders. In a work on the negotiation and ratification of the Japanese peace treaty, Bernard Cohen reports that some organization leaders approached State Department officials and not members of Congress and vice versa.[31] In a book describing an attempt by the government in 1958 to enlist support for its foreign economic policy, James N. Rosenau suggests that people in the executive branch see more of and hear more from "continentally-oriented" opinion leaders while congressmen are more in touch with those "segmentally oriented" (or more disposed to think in terms of locality, region, or interest group).[32] This means that, if statesmen in both branches do put much faith in letters and personal contacts, they may get quite different impressions of both actual and latent public opinion.

To what extent these men are guided by their estimates of public opinion is even less clear than how they arrive at these estimates. Officials in totalitarian states also pay close attention to public moods and expend a good deal of time and capital in testing opinion and trying to stimulate and orient it. A rationale can be constructed to explain why concern with public opinion in a democratic system is different. Congressmen have to be re-elected. To win votes, they have to respond at least to the more strongly felt wishes of their constituents. Although Presidents may not be concerned about their own re-election (and the Twenty-second Amendment guarantees that they seldom will be), they, too, have constituents. They bear a responsibility toward all followers

---

[30] Lewis Anthony Dexter, "What Do Congressmen Hear: The Mail," *ibid.*, XX (Spring, 1956), 16–27.

[31] Cohen, *The Political Process and Foreign Policy*, pp. 101–3.

[32] James N. Rosenau, *National Leadership and Foreign Policy: A Case Study in the Mobilization of Public Support* (Princeton, 1963), pp. 30–31, 331–62.

running for offices, and they are concerned about any pressures that affect congressmen. Hence it is arguable that they, too, would be responsive to the strongly felt wishes of the people.

But this rationale is based on traditional Enlightenment assumptions about democratic processes. The more that elections have been studied, the more doubtful these assumptions have become. Most voters apparently know very little about issues. The numbers with informed views on foreign policy are very few, and even among the informed, family background, party identification, religious affiliation, social class, locale of residence, and response to candidates' personalities or images seem at least as important as issues in determining voting behavior.[33] The fact is that there is almost no evidence to support the proposition that officeholders have to heed public opinion when deciding issues of foreign policy. Thus one might respond to Osokin that the government does not foster and manipulate public opinion because it does not need to do so.

Yet we would all feel instinctively that such an assertion is even more wide of the truth than Osokin's own. That public officials study the mail, read newspapers, and consult polls is itself evidence that they do care about public opinion. Looking back through American history, one can almost count on one's fingers the numbers of occasions when American statesmen made major decisions that they thought contrary to the public will. In the 1890's, Grover Cleveland refused to intervene in a civil war in Cuba even though he feared that the results might be Democratic defeats at the polls and conceivably the breakup of the Democratic party. Woodrow Wilson thought in the spring of 1916 (erroneously as it turned out) that the people were clamoring for war with Germany. He burst out to his private secretary, "I understand that the country wants action . . . but I will not be rushed into war, no matter if every last Congressman and Senator stands upon his hind legs and proclaims me a coward."[34] But it is clear in Cleveland's papers and Wilson's that both suffered agonies in taking stands they expected to be unpopular. Their sense of the statesmanlike forbade them to do what the public apparently wished, but their consciences told them they were servants of the people. The compulsion acting on them was, however,

[33] See the Berelson and Lazarsfeld studies cited in footnotes 10 and 14. Angus Campbell, Gerald Gurin, and Warren E. Miller, *The Voter Decides* (Evanston, Ill., 1954), assigns issue orientation a weight equal to party and candidate orientation but, in confirmation of Lazarsfeld's "cross-pressures" hypothesis, reports that the voter was likely to show up at the polls only if two of the three jibed. See also Key, *Public Opinion and American Democracy*, pp. 458–66.

[34] Joseph P. Tumulty, *Woodrow Wilson As I Know Him* (Garden City, 1921), p. 169. On the dilemma faced by Cleveland and his successor, see May, *Imperial Democracy*.

less external than internal. As participants in a democratic political system, they believed profoundly that they should represent, act for, and have their actions approved by, the mass of the citizenry. At least from the Jacksonian era onward, the idea that public policy should reflect mass opinion has had a powerful grasp on the mind of almost every man who has been prominent in American public life. Almost without exception, they have felt it their moral as well as political duty to act whenever possible in accord with public opinion. Paradoxically, the best response to Osokin is to say that the American tradition has validity because it is a tradition.

Such a conclusion is not necessarily reassuring. Most of the recent research on public opinion has had the effect of weakening this tradition by making more apparent the non-rational elements in individual opinions, the role of elites in shaping group opinion, and the fundamental difficulty of assessing effective public opinion. This research has also been fertile with new suggestions for possible manipulation of public opinion. The more statesmen absorb from social scientists, the more cynical they are apt to become about "the public will."

Government itself has been changing. The expert has become a much more important figure than in the past. The views of experts are accorded increasing weight, and it seems a natural predisposition of an expert to discount the views of the uninformed. George Kennan is the explicit and articulate exponent of the expert's viewpoint. In addition, foreign policy choices seldom seem so clear-cut now as they did, for example, in 1898 or 1914–17 or 1919 or 1939–41. Contemporary analysts stress the fact that decisions are often made incrementally.[35] A series of small decisions, few of which attract attention, leaves the government with a commitment that it cannot shirk or places it in a predicament in which it has little, if any, range of choice. All these conditions contribute to a drift away from the traditional belief. It may be that in time Americans will accept the view that prevailed in Europe until World War I—that foreign policy is an area where public opinion should not intrude.

Perhaps this is as it ought to be. Before it occurs, however, I hope that we can first learn something more about how our tradition works and has worked in practice. A historian reviewing social scientific research on public opinion is struck not only by the fact that historical and behavioral studies have seldom converged but by the fact that so few historians, political scientists, sociologists, or psychologists seem to have even borrowed perspectives from one another. The Harvard study

[35] See Charles E. Lindblom, "The Science of Muddling Through," *Public Administration Review*, XIX (Winter, 1959), 79–88.

on attitudes toward the Soviet Union, while in many ways a model, pays relatively little attention to social and historical pressures. The investigators looked for determinants in life histories, virtually disregarding the groups with which the individuals were affiliated, the impact of current events on them, or the assumptions and preconceptions they had absorbed or inherited. All but the very best sociological writing rests on implicit assumptions that are at variance with the findings of both psychology and history. One is that the attitudes and behavior of groups conform to patterns of rationality, as rationality is conceived by the sociologist. A second is that beliefs and actions can be explained in terms of factors discernible by contemporary observation, with scant regard to the effects of custom, tradition, inherited belief, and historical accident.[36]

Historians are even worse offenders. Not only in general surveys but even in detailed monographs, one can find elections characterized as, in effect, polls on the issues discussed by the candidates. Except in the few instances where intensive research has enforced caution, one also finds groups characterized as taking positions for reasons that the historian, from his own system of rationality, judges to have been logical or in their interest.

Little of the literature on the history of American foreign policy has taken account of the insights of behavioral scientists—not even of those, like James and Ross, who are now regarded as part of the nation's intellectual history. Like the State Department officials with whom Cohen talked, the typical monograph writer has equated public opinion with editorial opinion. One of Cohen's interviewees explained, "We are interested in seeing editorials, to see what is behind them, who wrote them, what weight they represent."[37] All too often, historical writing has not even bothered with distinctions such as these but has assumed that any editorial in any daily paper was a significant expression of public opinion. Although one of the unique assets of the historian is his ability to examine correspondence files, diaries, and other such intimate records, very few historical works have paid adequate attention to mail trends or to the presuppositions of statesmen or the methods they have used to assess public opinion.

Nor is it only mediocre or average writing that can be taken to task. One of the great works in modern historical scholarship is *The World Crisis and American Foreign Policy, 1937–1941*, by William L. Langer and S. Everett Gleason. Its fame is fully deserved, yet some of what it says about the relationship between public opinion and policy rests on ques-

---

[36] See especially Robert K. Merton, *Social Theory and Social Structure* (Glencoe, Ill., 1949), pp. 200–216, which contrasts American and European traditions in communications research.

[37] Cohen, *The Press and Foreign Policy*, p. 236.

tionable and unexamined assumptions. For example, the authors point out that a Gallup poll in October, 1941, showed that 70 per cent of the population deemed it more important to defeat Hitler than to stay out of the European war. At that very moment, the President was still worried about whether or not to press Congress for the repeal of the Neutrality Act that forbade American ships to enter a war zone or carry defensive armament. Here and elsewhere in the work, the authors implicitly criticize Roosevelt for lagging behind public opinion. What they fail to take into account are the President's own estimate of the value of polls and the quantitative judgments that could be made on the basis of other data. Roosevelt wrote Gallup after the October, 1941, poll: "I am a bit appalled by the percentage of people who have no clear idea of what the war is about." He doubted, in other words, that the opinion of the majority had adequate informational support. Mail to the White House included a large number of letters from mothers who did not want their sons in a war. For some of the population, opposition to any interventionist move was clearly an opinion high in saliency. While Roosevelt may well have accepted the estimate that 70 per cent of the population leaned one way, he could hardly jump to the conclusion that effective public opinion followed the same pattern.[38] A sense of qualitative distinctions that statesmen make is one of many insights that historians could borrow from social scientific research.

In appraising the worth of the traditional relationship between public opinion and policy, the various branches of social science can all borrow from one another. Also, with insights taken from various disciplines, scholars can perhaps find fruitful new areas for research. Just from the lacunae mentioned in this brief essay, some possibilities spring to mind.

Everyone concedes that there exist wide areas of consensus. The large majority of the public subscribes to certain propositions. For both opinion leaders and policy-makers, these propositions may serve as axioms.[39] But we know very little about how such consensus develops

[38] William L. Langer and S. Everett Gleason, *The World Crisis and American Foreign Policy,* Vol. II: *The Undeclared War, 1940–1941* (New York, 1953), pp. 752–53; Elliott Roosevelt (ed.), *F.D.R.: His Personal Letters, 1928–1945* (4 vols.; New York, 1947–48), II, 1349. See also Leila A. Sussmann, "FDR and the White House Mail," *Public Opinion Quarterly,* XX (Spring, 1956), 5–16, and "Mass Political Letter Writing in America," *ibid.,* XXIII (Summer, 1959), 203–12. On "effective" public opinion, see Herbert Blumer, "Public Opinion and Public Opinion Polling," in Bernard Berelson and Morris Janowitz (eds.), *Reader in Public Opinion and Communication* (Glencoe, Ill., 1950), pp, 594–602. For some suggestions as to how historians could make better use of survey research, see Robert A. Kann, "Public Opinion Research: A Contribution to Historical Method," *Political Science Quarterly,* LXXIII (Sept., 1958), 374–96.

[39] See Dahl, *Who Governs?* pp. 94–95, and Ernest R. May, "The Nature of Foreign Policy: The Calculated Versus the Axiomatic," *Daedalus,* XCI (Fall, 1962), 653–67.

or how opinion leaders or people in government apprehend its existence. To know more would obviously require study of survey results. It would also entail individual analyses which would seek to determine the sources of common ideas and the personality functions they perform. It would probably involve content analysis of popular periodicals, political speeches, press conferences, and the like. But research could only be inconclusive if it failed to take account of insights from political theory and from such fields as political and intellectual history and the history of education.

A related question has to do with the introduction of new ideas. In the comparatively recent past, the American public (or at least what Almond distinguishes as "the attentive public") has accepted ideas that would have seemed alien a short time before. Most notable are the ideas of prolonged conflict and deterrence. How did this happen? What, in other words, is the dynamism of consensus? And here the necessity of fusing historical and analytical work is even more clear, for an essential concern of historians is the how and why of change.[40]

And there are even more basic studies that might prove profitable. Practically all research on the subject has assumed that public opinion is an entity which can be described, dissected, and analyzed. But the very point to which we are driven in answering Osokin suggests that such an assumption is questionable.

Perhaps we ought to commence our research from a different premise. In *The Philosophy of "As If,"* Hans Vaihinger draws a distinction between hypotheses and fictions. Loosely speaking, the former are constructions subject to verification on the basis of evidence and experience, the latter are constructions which the mind invents in order to cope with the chaos that is reality. Perhaps public opinion should be conceived of, in

---

[40] On the sharp differences between the concept of deterrence and past concepts and on the apparent acceptance of the new concept by the public, see Samuel P. Huntington, *The Common Defense* (New York, 1962). Herbert Hyman in *Political Socialization* (Glencoe, Ill., 1959) suggested research on both consensus and change in consensus. There has been some microcosmic work on both subjects as, for example, David L. Sills, James A. Davis, John A. Michael, Martin L. Levin, and James S. Coleman, "Three 'Climate of Opinion' Studies," *Public Opinion Quarterly,* XXV (Winter, 1961), 571–610. See also the series of articles examining the processes by which doctors accept new drugs: Herbert Menzel and Elihu Katz, "Social Relations and Innovation in the Medical Profession: The Epidemiology of a New Drug," *Public Opinion Quarterly,* XIX (Winter, 1955–56), 339–52; James S. Coleman, Herbert Menzel, and Elihu Katz, "The Diffusion of an Innovation among Physicians," *Sociometry,* XX (December, 1957), 253–70, and "Social Processes in Physicians' Adoption of a New Drug," *Journal of Chronic Diseases,* IX (1959), 1–19; and Raymond A. Bauer, "Risk Handling in Drug Adoption: The Role of Company Preference," *Public Opinion Quarterly,* XXV (Winter, 1961), 546–59. Some interesting suggestions as to methods that might be used in such research are to be found in Charles E. Osgood, George J. Suci, and Percy H. Tannenbaum, *The Measurement of Meaning* (Urbana, Ill., 1957), and Sidney Verba, *Small Groups and Political Behavior: A Study of Leadership* (Princeton, 1961).

this sense, as a fiction. Perhaps at least some studies of it ought to begin not with what is observed but with the observers.

Research on voting behavior and research on public opinion have heretofore been interlaced. Perhaps the two ought to be separated. Ballots are objective realities which, like biological or geological entities, can be counted, compared, and categorized. But at the moment when a ballot is interpreted as a reflection of opinion, a number of elements subjective to the interpreter begin to enter in. Obviously, it would be extreme to say that at that moment the interpretation of reality becomes entirely subjective. Some degree of probability can certainly be assigned to such propositions as that a candidate can win votes by being a party regular or by taking stands that are urged on him by visible pressure groups. But the more removed a given issue is from ordinary partisanship or from the interests of quantifiable pressure groups (such as labor unions or Negroes), the more subjective becomes any judgment about what the ballot reflects.

Foreign policy issues are the extreme cases. Except on rare occasions, as in 1900 and 1920, such issues have not divided parties. Seldom have they gripped the attention of sizable pressure groups. Interpretations of public attitudes on foreign policy can almost never be drawn from election data. Here, therefore, the logical starting points for investigation seem to be precisely those that have been most neglected. How do men in government arrive at judgments about public opinion? To what extent are their judgments functions of individual personalities, backgrounds, and frames of reference? When, how, and in what ways do their ideas of actual or latent public opinion influence their thinking about substantive issues? Granting individual differences, are there distinctions in this regard within the government, say between the State Department and the Pentagon? All of these are questions that have scarcely been raised, let alone answered.

Our chief reason for believing that public opinion has influenced and does influence foreign policy is our knowledge that American statesmen have traditionally thought themselves responsible to, and supported or constrained by, some sort of general will. The national tradition is to accept as true the definition attributed to William of Malmesbury: *vox populi, vox Dei.* American political leaders have hearkened to the voice of the people as their seventeenth-century forebears did to the voice of God. Perhaps scholars, instead of listening for these voices themselves, ought to begin by inquiring what it is that these men thought they heard.

LOUIS MORTON

Civilians and Soldiers: Civil-Military Relations in the United States

Concern over the "military-industrialc omplex," or defense lobby, about which President Eisenhower warned the nation in his farewell address, and the controversy precipitated by the relief and resignation of General Edwin A. Walker, and before that of General MacArthur, remind us that even in the nuclear age the problem of civil-military relations is still with us, though in somewhat altered form and in a different context.

The relationship between the civilian authorities and the military leadership in a democracy is not a peculiarly American problem. The new nations of Asia and Africa and the Latin-American countries have yet to solve this problem. Simliar pressures have produced the same problems in other countries, and the recent history of the French army provides a grim warning of the consequences of failure to solve them. Over twenty years ago, Harold D. Lasswell first formulated the "garrison-state" hypothesis that the military class, whom he called the specialists on violence, was assuming a dominant position in the arena of world politics. Re-examining this hypothesis in a volume published in 1962, Professor Lasswell saw no reason to change his view and concluded that, unfortunately, the garrison hypothesis "provides a probable image of the past and future of our epoch."[1] If this is so, then our concern with the role of the military in our society is more than justified.

The problems of civil-military relations are not new; they have been with us since the founding of the Republic. Even before then, the colonists shared with their English brethren a traditional dislike and mistrust

LOUIS MORTON is Professor of History at Dartmouth College.

[1] Harold D. Lasswell, "The Garrison State Hypothesis Today," in Samuel P. Huntington (ed.), *Changing Patterns of Military Politics* (New York: Free Press of Glencoe, 1962), p. 67. For an excellent description of the crisis in French civil-military relations see the essay by Raoul Girardet, "Civil and Military Power in the Fourth Republic," in *ibid.*, pp. 121–50.

for standing armies.[2] But in the long perspective of history the problems of civil-military relations are of fairly recent origin. In ancient times, the line dividing the statesman and soldier was a very narrow one. More often, there was no line. And even in more recent times, when one man held the reins of power tightly in his own hands, the civil and military functions of the state were inseparable. Absolute rulers, men like Alexander, Caesar, Charlemagne, Genghis Khan, Cromwell, the French kings, Napoleon, not only presided over affairs of state but also led their armies in the field. There was no problem of civil-military relations, and what co-ordination was required between the political objectives of the state and the employment of military force took place in the person of the ruler. In a modern democracy the same result is achieved only imperfectly and with the greatest difficulty by complex institutional and organizational devices and the interplay of political forces, governmental processes, and public opinion.

The Founding Fathers understood very well the need for force in society and the inherent contradictions between the authoritarian and hierarchical nature of military institutions and a government based on consent of the governed.[3] Accepting the necessity for force, they had then to devise means for placing restraints on the military power without at the same time restricting it so closely that it would be unable to accomplish the purposes for which it was created. These purposes, it should be remembered, were internal as well as external; for the example of Shays' Rebellion in western Massachusetts was still fresh in their minds. But if the military power protected the state against danger, it posed dangers of its own. The Founding Fathers were only too well aware of these dangers, and their writings are full of allusions to Caesar and Cromwell. The problem before them was a difficult one: to create military institutions and forces consistent with a republican form of government and responsive to civilian authority. The fact that this government was a confederation only complicated the problem, for it meant that the military power would have to be divided between the federal government and the states.

How well the Founding Fathers accomplished their task is attested by the continuing vitality of the concept of civilian supremacy and the viability of American military traditions. To the federal government, they gave the power to wage war and to make peace; to create, maintain, and direct military forces, without any limit as to size, for the purpose of repelling invasion and preserving order; and to call forth the

[2] Colonial military institutions are described in Louis Morton, "The Origins of American Military Policy," *Military Affairs*, XXII, No. 2 (Summer, 1958), 75–82.

[3] See, for example, Hamilton's Essays Nos. 8 and 29, and Madison's Essay No. 41 in the *Federalist*.

militia when the necessity arose. To the states, the founders gave control over the militia, the citizen-soldiers who, according to the view then prevalent, would provide the bulk of the forces in any war. The militia was by this time an ancient institution, established by law in every colony and including on its rolls most able-bodied males between eighteen and forty-five. Finally, on the insistence of the ratifying conventions, the Founding Fathers guaranteed to each individual citizen, in the Second and Third Amendments, the right to bear arms (a guaranty against a despotic government that might seek to disarm its citizens), and the right to be protected against quartering of troops in their homes, except in a manner prescribed by law.

Thus was the military power divided as a check against unwarranted usurpation by either the state or the central government. Each would have its own forces, the state its militia, and the federal government a regular army and navy, but the state force could, when the Congress directed, be called into federal service. Moreover, the federal government was given authority to provide for organizing, arming, and disciplining the militia. The states were further prohibited from maintaining regular forces in time of peace, but were guaranteed protection by the federal government against invasion and domestic violence.

Within the central government, military power was divided between the legislative and executive branches in accordance with the principle of the separation of powers. No senator or representative, it was stipulated, could simultaneously hold any other office under the United States government, a stipulation that effectively barred military officers in the regular force from serving at the same time in Congress. To Congress was given the power of the purse, the power to raise and support an army and a navy, to make rules for their regulation, and to declare war. Appropriations for the army were limited under the Constitution to two years so that each new Congress would have the opportunity to review military policy, but no similar restriction was placed on naval funds, since no one feared an admiral on horseback.

The powers of Congress were broad, but not nearly as sweeping as those given to the President, who was made commander in chief of the army and navy as well as of the militia when it was called into federal service. It is important to note here that the President was not given command of the military forces as an additional function but was vested with an office and a title carrying with it a blanket authority limited only by the power of Congress to impeach. And it is not without significance that while the President's power was virtually unlimited, congressional authority was carefully defined.

The arrangements made in the Constitution for the control of military forces clearly reflected the late eighteenth-century conception of war and the role of force in society, as well as the American tradition, already old, of reliance on the militia rather on a professional army. Since these conditions have been altered or modified with the passage of time, it has been argued that the constitutional provisions relating to the armed forces are not only irrelevant but may even constitute an obstacle to achievement of the purposes for which they were intended.[4] Thus the separation of power between the executive and legislative authorities, it is asserted, actually weakens civilian supremacy, as does the division between the states and the central government. "For the purposes of objective civilian control," writes Professor Huntington, "the American Constitution was drafted at just the wrong time in history. Twenty-five years or more later, its clauses about military affairs might well have been written differently."[5]

Certainly there is much truth in this assertion. By dividing authority over the militia between the state and federal governments, the Constitution undoubtedly made a single effective control difficult. And by playing off Congress against the President, as the air force has done in recent years in the matter of the B-70, the military can actually weaken civilian supremacy. It is true also that the Second and Third Amendments to the Constitution are without much meaning today and the militia as it was understood by the Founding Fathers is an outmoded institution. Nor will anyone quarrel seriously with the assertion that the two-year limit on congressional appropriations for the army is an anachronism in a day when the creation of a weapons system from the blueprint stage to production may take as long as five years or more. But when these restrictions become irksome, means are found to circumvent them, and I can see no great advantage, and perhaps some disadvantages, in rewriting the offending clauses of the Constitution. The fact that the President possesses and has on occasion exercised the power to initiate hostilities by executive action scarcely justifies modifying the congressional power to declare war.

Despite the changes that time has wrought in the work of the Founding Fathers, the principle of civilian supremacy remains firmly fixed in tradition and practice. As a matter of fact, it is remarkable that after 170 years so many of the constitutional provisions relating to military force are still relevant. The concept of the militia as a local force of citizen-soldiers ready to spring to the defense of the nation at a moment's notice may be outmoded, but the National Guard stands today

---

[4] See, for example, Samuel P. Huntington, *The Soldier and the State* (Cambridge, Mass.: Harvard University Press, 1957), chap. 7; and Walter Millis, *The Constitution and the Common Defense* (New York: Fund for the Republic, 1959), pp. 21–24, where the author rewrites the military clauses of the Constitution in modern language.

[5] Huntington, "Civilian Control and the Constitution," *American Political Science Review*, L, No. 3 (September, 1956), 679.

as heir to that tradition, a military force of the state government, subject to the orders of the governor through officers appointed by him. Congress continues to scrutinize the military budget and through this power exercises a measure of influence on strategic programs and on the size and structure of the military establishment.

From the start, the principal instrument of civilian supremacy and control was the commander-in-chief clause. In combining the civilian functions of the chief executive with the military powers of the commander in chief, the Founding Fathers, perhaps unwittingly, created one of the most powerful offices in the world. Most Presidents have jealously guarded these powers, expanding them as the necessity arose, and adding to the existing machinery for control as the problems of war became more complex. Washington, who had a rare talent for thinking in both military and political terms, understood the military requirements of the new Republic and set the precedents for the exercise of his authority as commander in chief. But President Jefferson, who had had no military experience, could see little value in a permanent military establishment, whether army or navy, asserting in his first annual message to Congress in 1801 that it was neither needful nor safe to keep a standing army in time of peace.[6]

Jacksonian democracy confirmed and extended the Jeffersonian rather than the Washingtonian concept of the role of force. To the true democrat of the 1820's and 1830's, a professional class of military men represented a parasitic element in society performing no useful function. Any good American, it was firmly believed, was a match for troops anywhere in the world. Had not Jackson, a militia general, defeated the cream of the British army at the Battle of New Orleans? On this basis there was no real need for a standing force, except to perform the unpleasant tasks no one else would perform. "Antipathy toward war," wrote Henry Adams of the early years of the nineteenth century, "ranked first among the political traits" of Americans.[7] It was in keeping with this spirit that President Jackson, in his first inaugural address in March, 1829, declared his intention to abide by "that salutary lesson of political experience which teaches that the military should be held subordinate to the civil power." And he reinforced the democratic faith in the simple virtues by asserting further his belief that the bulwark of the nation's defense lay in its militia. A million armed free men, he declared, "possessed of the means of war, can never be conquered by

[6] James D. Richardson (comp.), *Messages and Papers of the Presidents* (New York, 1897), I, 317.

[7] Henry Adams, *History of the United States of America during the Second Administration of James Madison* (New York, 1891), III, 226.

a foreign foe."[8] Almost a hundred years later, Wilson was to utter virtually the same sentiment, despite the fact that experience had already worn this cliché thin.[9] Jackson was on safer ground; he had no need to employ force, though he was not reluctant to do so on several occasions, and he was therefore able to keep the army small and under tight control. Wilson was not so fortunate, and his administration witnessed a remarkable growth in the power of the military.

The constitutional clause conferring the commander's mantle on the President is noteworthy for its brevity. Its meaning is clear, yet unclear. For nowhere are the powers granted under this clause defined. That is its great strength, and each President has had to define it in his own way. Can a President lead troops into battle? Can he make strategy and order generals to follow his plan? Can he relieve officers in the field and actively direct operations? Or must he sit at home and concern himself only with the civilian side of war? Washington did not. When the farmers along the Pennsylvania frontier rebelled against the excise tax on whiskey in 1794, Washington assumed personal command of the militia called out to meet the emergency. James Madison, too, took to the field when the British threatened the capital in 1814 and, though he was more a hindrance than a help, was present at the Battle of Bladensburg. And in the war with Mexico, President Polk pretty well told his generals where he wanted them to go and what he wanted them to do. He had his troubles with the generals, as did Truman and Eisenhower (himself a general), but there was never any real question about who was in charge.

No President exercised the war powers granted by the Constitution as broadly as did Lincoln, and none kept so close to affairs on the battlefield. Until he was satisfied that he had found in Grant a general who would fight, he kept a tight control over his major commanders and relieved them when they failed to produce the results he sought. He has been criticized often for "interfering" with the conduct of military operations, but this, I think, is an unfair criticism. It was his constitutional responsibility to see that the war was vigorously prosecuted; when it was not, it was his duty to relieve the officers responsible for failure. How seriously he took this responsibility emerges clearly, as does the quality of the man, I think, in his letter to General Hooker appointing him Commander of the Army of the Potomac:

Of course I have done this upon what appears to me sufficient reason, and yet I think it best for you to know that there are some things in regard to which

---

[8] Both statements are from the First Inaugural, March, 1829, Richardson, *op. cit.*, III, 1000.

[9] See Wilson's Second Annual Message to Congress, December, 1914.

I am not quite satisfied with you. I believe you to be a brave and skillful soldier, which, of course, I like. I also believe you do not mix politics with your profession, in which you are right. You have confidence in yourself, which is a valuable, if not an indispensable quality. You are ambitious, which, within reasonable bounds, does good rather than harm . . . I have heard, in such a way as to believe it, of your recently saying that both the Army and the Government needed a dictator. Of course it was not for this, but in spite of it, that I have given you the command. Only those generals who gain successes can set up as dictators. What I now ask of you is military success, and I will risk the dictatorship. . . .[10]

Lincoln did not have to worry about the dictatorship, because Hooker did not win any victories.

The period from the Civil War to the War with Spain has been described as the "Dark Age" for the army. The great Civil War army was demobilized in less than a year and remained at a strength of approximately 25,000 thereafter. In a society that was rapidly becoming industrialized, the army's main function was to fight Indians on the frontier. Neglected, often abused, and scattered in small detachments among a large number of widely separated posts, the army was isolated from the mainstream of American life. It was during these years that it became a truly professional corps, with officers who had an image of themselves as non-partisan, non-political instruments of the state, practictioners of the science of war in the same way that doctors were practitioners of the science of medicine.

At the turn of the twentieth century, the United States stood on the threshold of world power and, under the leadership of Elihu Root, set about the task of modernizing and reorganizing its military forces. In 1903, the general staff system was established in the army and a chief of staff replaced the old commanding general. An Army War College was created to train officers for the general staff and for high command, and for the first time in over a hundred years a militia act was passed setting up the National Guard.

None of these actions affected the basic structure established in 1789. The tradition of civilian supremacy remained as strong as ever, despite the fact that the army and navy had become increasingly professional and the high command more centralized. One could argue, rather, that these developments had strengthened, not weakened, civilian control. To those who had opposed these reforms as opening the way to military dictatorship, Secretary Root had replied: "No one ever knew of the Army seeking to make itself a political agent. No one ever knew of the American army seeking to make itself a Praetorian guard to set up a

[10] *Lincoln's Complete Works* (New York, 1905). VIII, 207.

president or an emperor."[11] And speaking for the navy, John D. Long declared in 1903: "Ours is a civil and not a military government. The President is a civilian . . . ; the heads of the Army and Navy departments are civilians. The fundamental principle of our Constitution is that the military is subordinate to the civil function."[12] Lord Bryce, a perceptive observer of American institutions, confirmed both judgments from his detached position as a British subject. "Caeserism," he wrote, "is the last danger likely to menace America. In no nation is civil order more stable. None is more averse to the military spirit."[13] One wonders whether he would have made the same judgment today.

Civil-military relations involve more than civilian supremacy, an issue that was never seriously in doubt. An effective working relationship between statesmen and soldiers to co-ordinate the political and military elements of policy is also implied. In the early years of the Republic, when the military played a comparatively small part in the life of the nation and when its interests and responsibilities were limited, the need for such a relationship was not vital and the absence of mechanisms to achieve it was scarcely noted. But when the United States acquired colonies far from its shores and moved out into the world arena, it became evident to some that force, or the threat of force, was an essential element in our relations with other powers. Foreign policy could scarcely overlook the military factor, and political commitments without the force to back them up might well lead to humiliating defeat.

Recognition of the importance of political-military co-ordination does not mean that civilian supremacy has lost all meaning. Recent events testify that this is not so, but it was evident by 1900 that civilian supremacy was no longer the main problem. The principle was accepted, and the institutions and traditions that gave it force had been tested by time. The problem rather was to define the proper role of the military in the transformed America of the twentieth century and to insure that the military as well as the political factors in any situation were fully considered. It was the task of succeeding administrations to solve this problem through organizational devices and political processes within the framework of the American system of government.

The organizational pattern, as we have seen, was set by Elihu Root, whose chief, Theodore Roosevelt, understood better than most of his contemporaries and many of his successors the need for blending the political and military ingredients of policy. Thus, when Root with his naval colleague agreed to establish a Joint Board to consider matters of

[11] Elihu Root, *The Military and Colonial Policy of the United States* (Cambridge, Mass.: Harvard University Press, 1916), p. 18.

[12] John D. Long, *The New American Navy* (New York, 1903), II, 182.

[13] James Bryce, *The American Commonwealth* (rev. ed.; New York, 1937), II, 623.

interest to both services, they found strong support in the White House. This Joint Board, which ultimately became the Joint Chiefs of Staff, consisted of four members of the army's newly created General Staff and the navy's General Board, including the ranking members of each service. At first it proved an effective instrument of policy and spoke with authority in the highest councils of the nation, but after a disagreement in 1907 with President Roosevelt its influence declined visibly.[14] The State Department, never enthusiastic about co-operation with the military, saw no need to consult with the generals and admirals, and by the time of World War I, the Joint Board had become virtually defunct.

The status of the military profession in the United States in the period between the two world wars sank as low as it had ever been. The four-million-man army created during the war was demobilized as quickly as the Union Army had been after the Civil War. Disillusion with war, pacificism, and economic depression all combined during the 1920's and 1930's to keep military appropriations low and the military officer in a subordinate role. Though the military used these years to absorb the lessons of the war and strengthen their organization, including the revival of the Joint Board, their efforts to secure a larger voice in the determination of policies were in vain. When, in 1922, the two service secretaries proposed a closer relationship between the military and the State Department, Secretary of State Hughes rebuffed them politely but firmly. Evidently Hughes read the proposal, perhaps correctly, as an effort by the Joint Board to secure a voice in the determination of foreign policy, and he was by no means disposed to grant it this right.[15]

The effects of this lack of co-ordination between the diplomatic and military agencies of the government before World War II may be observed in many areas, but nowhere more strikingly than in China. American troops, you will remember, had gone to China after the Boxer Uprising in 1900, and ever since the early 1920's the War Department had been trying to secure the consent of the State Department to their withdrawal. But each time the Secretary of War raised this question, he was turned down. Every Secretary of State from Hughes to Hull consistently maintained the priority of State Department interests over those of the military. Even after the Japanese had moved into North China in 1937, the State Department refused to permit the army to evacuate its troops, though their position had clearly become untenable. Finally, the army decided to appeal directly to the President. In a memorandum that deserves to stand as a milestone in the development

[14] For the early history of the Joint Board, see Louis Morton, "Interservice Cooperation and Political-Military Collaboration, 1900–1938," in Harry L. Coles (ed.), *Total War and Cold War* (Columbus: Ohio State University Press, 1962), pp. 131–61.

[15] For description of this incident, see *ibid.*, pp. 143–47.

of political-military co-ordination, Louis Johnson, then Assistant Secretary of War and later Secretary of Defense, laid his case before Mr. Roosevelt in these terms:

I find that this action of the State Department in ignoring military advice has been characteristic of its attitude for many years past. . . . My investigation discloses that this is an attitude not assumed by the foreign office of any other nation. On the contrary, none embarks upon a foreign policy having any military implications without giving the fullest consideration to the advice of the responsible military authorities. . . . May I respectfully ask that you consider directing the Secretary of State to afford an opportunity to the War Department to express its views upon all matters having a military implication, immediate or remote.[16]

This was strong language and the record does not disclose what action, if any, Franklin Roosevelt took. But we do know that within six months the army was out of China.

Just before World War II, as the danger to the United States loomed larger, President Roosevelt took steps to give the military an increasingly larger role in the making of policy. In 1938 he established the Standing Liaison Committee, consisting of the Under Secretary of State, the Chief of Staff, and the Chief of Naval Operations. The next year, he placed the Joint Board directly under his immediate supervision, thereby enhancing the power and prestige of that body.[17] Finally, in 1941, he began to meet more or less regularly with the State, War, and Navy Secretaries, the Chief of Staff, and the Chief of Naval Operations to discuss the many problems of national defense. This group, known informally as the War Council, became in effect a co-ordinating body for foreign and military policy.[18]

During World War II the roles of the military services and the State Department were reversed, an arrangement that was as undesirable from the point of view of long-range national interests as the earlier situation had been. For the military, nurtured in the tradition of the separation of political and military matters, viewed all questions from a purely military point of view. As John Davies, a veteran foreign service officer remarked in 1943: "Most of our officers want the job accomplished as soon as possible, with a minimum of fuss over international political and economic issues, which they regard as of secondary

[16] Memorandum from Johnson for the President, Sept. 1, 1937, cited in Louis Morton, "Army and Marines on China Station: A Study in Politico-Military Rivalry," *Pacific Historical Review*, February, 1960.

[17] Military Order, July 5, 1939.

[18] Mark S. Watson, *Chief of Staff: Prewar Plans and Preparations* (Washington, 1950), pp. 89-91.

importance. Political and economic questions, they feel, can be discussed and decided after the defeat of the Axis."[19]

This view represents an entirely justifiable basis for civil-military relations, but its validity under the conditions of modern war rests upon the willingness of the political authorities to exercise their own responsibilities by providing the guidelines for strategy. When, as in World War II, civilian officials failed to do so, the result was a military strategy largely unrelated to political objectives. And whether they wanted to or not, the military had a large influence in political matters, for in war virtually all important decisions have political implications. But the point is that military considerations were predominant and were accepted as such by the political as well as the military authorities. "The needs of military strategy," General Marshall told a committee of influential senators, "must dominate the conduct of the war."[20] And no one on the committee challenged him. The United States fought World War II with little awareness of political objectives and with a single-minded devotion to the idea of military victory. Only in the person of the President was military strategy related to long-range political goals. To all intents and purposes the State Department sat on the sidelines throughout most of the war, while the military occupied the center of the stage.

Accustomed to leadership during the war and basking in the sunshine of victory, the military naturally continued to exercise a strong influence on policy in the postwar period. Significantly, it was the War and Navy Departments rather than the State Department which shaped the pattern of political-military co-ordination embodied in the National Security Act of 1947. With this act, which established a separate air force, a Department of Defense, the CIA and the National Security Council, the structure of our present system for integrating the various elements involved in the formulation of policy was largely completed. Ever since then, it must be added, we have been tinkering with this machinery in the hope of improving the process by which policy decisions are made, but with little success. For over a year, a committee of Congress subjected the entire national security organization to the most searching examination and explored every proposal for its improvement, only to arrive at the conclusion that the solution to the problems of political-military co-ordination depends not on organization but on the quality and understanding of the men assigned to this task, and on

[19] "Policy Conflicts among the United Nations," paper by John Davies, Sept. 17, 1943, included in a memo from General Magruder to General Roberts, Dec. 15, 1943.

[20] Quoted in Maurice Matloff, *Strategic Planning for Coalition Warfare, 1943–1944* (Washington, 1957), p. 111.

their willingness to subordinate the parochial interests of their agency or service to the larger requirements of policy.[21]

It should be clear by now, I think, that whatever the institutional forms and wherever the locus of responsibility, co-ordination of the political and military considerations that go into the making of national security policy is not easily achieved. It is not simply a matter of balancing one set of factors against another. The problem is much more complex than that and involves a number of questions not easily answered. In the first place, it is by no means a simple matter to distinguish between political and military factors at the highest level. Even if it were, how much weight should we attach to each? Which should govern—the political or the military? What do we do when the two of them clash?

The conventional picture, the stereotype of political-military co-ordination, one widely accepted in the military and derived from Clausewitz' dictum about war as a continuation of politics, is that policy governs military strategy. It is as simple as that, and reads as follows: The civilian policy-maker lays down the guidelines, states what the national objectives and goals are; and then the military men make the plans and shape the forces to secure these objectives. "In our country," wrote the planners of the General Staff as far back as 1915, "public opinion estimates the situation, statecraft shapes the policy, while the duty of executing it devolves upon the military and naval departments."[22]

This kind of picture, I would suggest, is oversimplified—so oversimplified as to be misleading. National objectives often conflict with each other and, in any case, are not readily defined. Even if they were, it is not always desirable to spell them out. Nor is it always possible politically to provide the forces required to support a given policy in the last extremity or even to define clearly under what contingencies force should be used. Sometimes military factors dominate; at other times political considerations prevail. Hard and fast rules, elaborate plans, may limit action rather than facilitate it and thus lead to inflexibility.

The consequences of a failure to appreciate fully and to assess accurately the impact of political decisions on military strategy, or conversely of strategy on policy, can be far-reaching. To cite only one example, consider the effect of the Allied demand for unconditional surrender in World War II. This was a political goal set by the political

[21] *Final Statement of Senator Henry M. Jackson*, Subcommittee on National Policy Machinery of the Committee on Government Operations, U.S. Senate, Nov. 15, 1961, 87 Congress, 1 sess.

[22] *A Proper Military Policy for the United States*, War College Division, General Staff, U.S. Army, September, 1915.

authorities, and it was made, so far as we know, without any reference whatsoever to the military. Yet it had enormous implications for the military planners. It imposed upon them the requirement for a strategy of total destruction. In the case of Japan such a strategy was both unnecessary and unrealistic. Japan was already defeated and seeking a way out of the war. And we knew it. Acceptance of the Imperial system might have produced a Japanese surrender entirely satisfactory to the Allies, as it ultimately did, but the unconditional surrender formula could not be changed so late in the war. We had become the victims of our own propaganda. Our policy was frozen, and so the strategists went ahead with their plans for an invasion of the Japanese home islands, even at the risk of enormously high casualties. This was the box we were in when the atomic bomb was successfully tested over the white sands of New Mexico. The result you already know. Given the political aims, the strategy designed to secure these aims, and the estimate of casualties expected, what other course could President Truman have taken?

Korea offers another striking illustration of the way in which military considerations may affect political goals. In fact, one might well make a case for the view that our political objectives in Korea—which are not easy to pin down—shifted with the fortunes of our forces on the battlefield, and that military considerations had as much or more to do with our actions than the political goals set by the policy-makers.

It was no accident that MacArthur's mission was enlarged in September, 1950, to allow him to drive northward across the thirty-eighth parallel, although he had been prohibited from doing this earlier, for it was in that month—September, 1950—that he turned the enemy's flank at Inchon and forced on him a general retreat into North Korea. The return to a more restricted objective two months later, it should be noted, came after the large-scale Chinese intervention in November and the subsequent withdrawal of MacArthur's forces.

The Chinese, too, shifted their objectives with their military fortunes. Their inability to push the UN forces into the sea led *them* to place limits on their own political aims and undoubtedly made them receptive to, and perhaps eager for, negotiation. Thus, in both cases it was the military means that shaped political ends rather than the other way around, as is so often thought.

A limited war like Korea is particularly rich in the lessons of political-military co-ordination, especially for the American people with their penchant for making their wars moral crusades, fought with total means and for total objectives. By its very nature, limited war places a premium on political considerations and on solutions short of military victory. Limited war also requires closer controls over the commander in the field and places restrictions on his freedom of action. The result is to increase greatly the potentialities for disagreements, irritations, and sharp clashes. The Cold War, that uneasy state that is neither peace nor war, does the same and imposes even greater strains on the relationships between civilian policy-makers and military commanders.

It is not surprising, therefore, that the decade of the 1950's should see the emergence of a group of military dissidents, outspoken in their criticism of the existing administration and allied with similar politically dissident groups, usually those on the extreme right. Military men were now involved more intimately than ever before in the making of policy, partly as a result of the role of the United States in world affairs and partly because of the revolution in military technology. Such military men were faced with problems of unprecedented magnitude for which there were no clear-cut solutions—at least none that were politically acceptable. By training, the military man seeks clear objectives and decisive actions. Like the scientist, whose position now is somewhat similar to that of his uniformed colleague in an earlier period, the military man has essentially a problem-solving kind of mentality, and some of the problems he faced now were insoluble and clearly called not for decisive action but, rather, for the opposite.

There was ample evidence also of military dissatisfaction with the role assigned them in the formulation of policy. This dissatisfaction stemmed in part, I think, from the military conception of co-ordination. In 1922, when they suggested that State Department representatives should sit on the Joint Board, and in 1945–46, when they advocated the establishment of an agency like the National Security Council, the military leaders were thinking in terms of an agency, somewhat on the model of the Joint Chiefs of Staff, in which they would deliberate as equals. And in wartime, of course, they expected that their views would prevail. What happened was that the military were relegated to the position of furnishing advice when asked—a position that some found difficult to accept. Still, it was a situation they had helped to create, and it is hard to see how it could have been otherwise under our system of government. Foreign policy belongs to the State Department and the White House. And the military, whose views dominated during World War II and for some years thereafter, had now taken their place as partners, and by no means the most important partners, in determining the relationship of the United States to the rest of the world and in shaping our national security policy. The civilian, not the military man, was the general in the Cold War.

Under these conditions and faced by problems that defied solution, it was not unreasonable to expect that the frustrations which produced extremist groups in our political life should also appear among the military. General MacArthur's experience in Korea was not an isolated one; his position and prestige only made it seem so. General Ridgway and General Clark, who succeeded him, were as unhappy with their situation in Korea as MacArthur, and Clark was as outspoken in his criticism. The strain of fighting a limited and unpopular war in which there was no prospect of victory and where military action was severely limited found its outlet in attacks on the civilian leadership—attacks which the political opposition happily encouraged. The strain of the Cold War has had the same effect and, though the number of officers involved is small, this criticism is significant, for it constitutes essentially an assault upon civilian supremacy. Whether such dissidence takes this form, or the form of political indoctrination of troops, or so-called "strategy seminars," it seems to me to stem from the same cause: an inability or unwillingness to accept the prevailing political judgment and to work within the accepted pattern of civil-military relations. In this sense, it represents a dangerous trend that may produce a strong public reaction unfavorable in the long run to the military. Prudence would dictate, therefore, that the military profession reject its more radical elements lest irreparable harm be done. There is, fortunately, every reason to believe it is doing so. In the final analysis, the best guaranty of civilian supremacy lies in the strong tradition of the professional corps itself that its role in American society is to serve the state, regardless of party, program, or policy.

HANS J. MORGENTHAU

The American Political Legacy

Is THERE an American political legacy distinct from that of other nations? Two schools of thought answer this question in the negative. They assume that American politics is really no different from European politics and that the claim that there is a distinctive quality to American politics is unfounded. The first of these schools of thought arose in the thirties under the impact of an economic crisis which appeared to belie the claim that America, in contrast to Europe, was free of class division and class conflict. As Professor Louis M. Hacker, who has changed his mind in the meantime, put it in 1933:

> The historical growth of the United States, in short, was not unique; merely in certain particulars and for a brief time, it was different from the European pattern largely because of the processes of settlement. With settlement achieved — ... class (not sectional!) lines solidified, competitive capitalism converted into monopolistic capitalism under the guidance of the money power, and imperialism the ultimate destiny of the nation—the United States once again was returning to the main stream of European institutional development. Only by a study of the origins and growth of American capitalism and imperialism can we obtain insight into the nature and complexity of the problems confronting us today. And I am prepared to submit that perhaps the chief reason for the absence of this proper understanding was the futile hunt for a unique "American spirit. ..."[1]

More recently, another school of thought has argued against the distinctiveness of the American political legacy on grounds taken from intellectual history. That school assumes that the ideas which went into the making of American politics were all European ideas and that America really contributed nothing of substance to them. Yet while it is true

HANS J. MORGENTHAU is Professor of Political Science and Modern History at the University of Chicago.

[1] Louis M. Hacker, "Sections—or Classes," in George Rogers Taylor, *The Turner Thesis concerning the Role of the Frontier in American History* (Boston, D. C. Heath & Co., 1949), p. 64.

that economic classes exist in America and that the substance of American political thought stems from Europe, it is no less true that American classes are different from European ones and that the political ideas of Europe have performed in America different functions from the ones they did on the continent of their origin. As the immigrants who brought them were transformed by life in America, so were the political ideas and institutions of Europe. They were transformed into something new and unique. All of American history and the experiences of contemporary American life militate against the denial of a distinct American political legacy.

The early Americans and the onlookers in other nations both were convinced that the American political experiment had a unique character, that it was something which had never been tried before, and that its success or failure would determine the political future of humanity. Thomas Paine could claim that the American Revolution was not made for Americans alone but for all humanity, that it had universal significance:

She [America] made a stand, not for herself only, but for the world, and looked beyond the advantages herself could receive. Even the Hessian, though hired to fight against her, may live to bless his defeat; and England, condemning the viciousness of its Government, rejoice in its miscarriage. . . . The Revolutions which formerly took place in the world had nothing in them that interested the bulk of mankind. They extended only to a change of persons and measures, but not of principles, and rose or fell among the common transactions of the moment.[2]

While such a claim might be dismissed or at least explained in terms of patriotism, it is of profound significance that throughout the eighteenth and nineteenth centuries other nations accepted this claim and looked at the American experiment as a model to be emulated by other nations, as a standard by which the political development of other nations was to be judged.

On the occasion of the Fourth of July, 1956, a Russian writer, replying in *The New Times* to the accusation that the Soviet Union was exporting its revolution, paid the United States the compliment of saying that it was the United States itself which had started the export of revolution in 1776. "All the peoples of the world, each in their own way, were affected at the time by the Fourth of July and felt its consequences."[3] In the reactionary Russian press of the nineteenth century, he added, the word "American" was synonymous with "revolutionary."

There is, then, among Americans and both friendly and hostile on-

[2] Thomas Paine, *The Rights of Man* (New York: E. P. Dutton & Co., 1951), pp. 151, 154.

[3] *New York Times*, July 3, 1956.

lookers a consensus about the distinctive character of the American political inheritance, and there remains only one question for us to discuss: In what does this heritage consist? What are its distinctive qualities? What sets it apart from other political traditions?

The American political tradition has two main characteristics, both of which were consciously created by the Founding Fathers and have been consciously or unconsciously, as the case might have been, applied to political realities throughout American history. The first is the conception of limited government. The Constitutional Convention at Philadelphia and the *Federalist* papers are dominated by the fear of absolute political power. What we have come to call American democracy was originally an attempt, very much in the British tradition starting with Magna Carta, reaffirmed and extended in the Glorious Revolution, consummated in the Reform legislation of the nineteenth and twentieth centuries, to limit the powers of the executive branch through institutions manned by elective officers. The original conception of democracy, as developed by the British tradition, did not understand democracy as government of the people, by the people, and for the people; it sought rather to establish a government whose powers were limited through the majority rule expressed both in the votes of Parliament and in the elections to Parliament.

In America, the same function of limiting the powers of government is performed by the federal system dividing the functions of government between the federal and state governments, by the presidential veto, judicial review of legislative and executive acts, equal representation of states in the Senate regardless of population, disproportionate representation of rural constituencies in state legislatures and Congress, seniority rule, rule by committee, and filibuster in Congress. All these institutions and practices run counter to the idea of majority rule. They seek to forestall a government ruling through the majority without qualifications and limitations. They seek to establish a government whose powers are ultimately controlled by the majority through periodical elections, but whose day-by-day operations are not so controlled.

The other distinctive characteristic of the American political tradition is generally called the "pluralism of America." It is at that point that the modern denials of a distinct American political tradition have at least the semblance of a case. For it is true that the United States has never been committed to one substantive political philosophy, as for instance France or the Soviet Union is today. From the very beginning, American political thought assumed that out of what Mr. Justice Holmes called the competition of the market, that is to say, the competition of different political ideas and philosophies, the truth would emerge, and that no particular group had a monopoly of political truth, that the best one could hope for was an approximation to the political truth through the free and equal interplay of intellectual, social, and political forces.

This pluralism has the additional function of limiting the powers of government. For it is exactly by virtue of this pluralism based on geography, religion, ethnic loyalties, economic interests, urban versus rural communities, and so forth—it is by virtue of a whole network of pluralistic juxtapositions that it is impossible for any one single interest, one single sub-society in America, to impose itself upon the whole. The technique of lobbying, not always providing an elevating spectacle of disinterested dedication to the common good, is an expression of this deeply ingrained pluralism of American society. There is nothing wrong with lobbying, that is to say, with one parochial group trying to impress the importance of its interests upon the government, as long as this group is forced to compete in the market place with different lobbying groups. What runs counter to the American political tradition, that is, the pluralism of American society, is a monopolistic or quasi-monopolistic position of one particular interest to the exclusion of all others.

What is true of domestic politics is also true of foreign policy, and it is here even more strikingly true: the dominance of the idea that the American experiment in politics constitutes a radical departure from political tradition, that the American experiment introduced into the political experience of mankind an entirely novel, unheard-of element. You have only to read Washington's Farewell Address, written in good measure by Hamilton, the most eminent of American ghost-writers, in order to see how profoundly convinced the Founding Fathers were of the unique and unprecedented position which the United States held among the nations and of the radically different policies that were to follow from that position. It was generally believed, not only in the eighteenth century but throughout the nineteenth as well and almost to the beginning of World War II, that the United States was free from the risks and liabilities with which other nations had to cope in their relations with each other. The United States was fortunate in that it was a continental power without any neighbor strong enough to threaten its interests, let alone its existence. It was for this reason that the United States could embark upon what one might call an abstentionist foreign policy, which outside the Western Hemisphere was hardly a foreign policy at all; for the United States had no interests outside the Western Hemisphere, and within the Western Hemisphere it had only one interest: to be left alone in order to be able to expand at will. The Monroe Doctrine is the expression of this negative attitude toward foreign policy.

Both in domestic politics and foreign policy this heritage of American politics, this American political legacy, is challenged and is put into question. This is of course obvious on the international scene, and it is less obvious, but no less real, on the domestic scene.

On the international scene we realized, and to our credit we realized very quickly after the end of World War II, to what extent the isolation which we enjoyed in the eighteenth and nineteenth centuries was an ephemeral historic episode by no means intrinsic in the American existence, but the result of the actual remoteness of the centers of world politics from the Western Hemisphere. With the successive revolutions in communication and transportation, starting in the first half of the nineteenth century with the invention of the railroads, this remoteness was bound to disappear, and with that disappearance the whole nature of American foreign policy was bound to change.

In 1938, the Congress of the United States was still capable of passing the so-called neutrality legislation inspired by a strictly isolationist concept of American foreign policy and based upon the assumption that the prohibition of loans and of the transportation of war matériel in American bottoms to belligerents would prevent the involvement of America in a second world war. Yet ten years later, in the spring of 1947, in what has been called "The Fifteen Weeks," American foreign policy was refashioned in the light of new experiences. The government of the United States declared the eastern frontiers of the United States to be at the Rhine, stationed American troops in virtual permanence in the center of Europe, and committed itself through the Marshall Plan and the Truman Doctrine to the containment of communism around the globe with economic, military, and political means. Suddenly what since the beginning of our history had been regarded as the proper American foreign policy was proved to be inadequate and in need of reformulation and adaptation to new conditions.

Here we are face to face with the fundamental political problem with which this generation must come to terms at home and abroad, that is, how to reformulate and adapt the traditional concepts of American politics to conditions of unprecedented novelty. This is the great creative task which America must perform today and tomorrow. It must not deny the existence of an American political legacy or assume that this American political legacy has become meaningless for the contemporary world. But rather it must separate that which is historically conditioned in this legacy from that which contains a perennial political truth and adapt this perennial political truth to the conditions of the day.

Let us then very briefly and, in a sense, superficially, survey the theoretical and practical consequences of that task. The predominant conception of American politics at home and abroad which underlies its two main characteristics, limited government and pluralism, can be defined in three words: equality in freedom. What the settlers of the seventeenth and eighteenth centuries sought to establish on the North American continent was a political, social, and economic system which would present every individual with an equal opportunity for advancement under the conditions of freedom. The Founding Fathers sought to establish political institutions strong enough to protect the freedom of the individual but not so strong as to be able to destroy it.

The social and political history of America is the story of a succession of attempts to achieve equality in freedom, each failure calling forth a new effort with means adapted to new circumstances, each crisis being responded to with a new affirmation and new, however partial, achievement. Equality under the condition of unfreedom can exist in a totalitarian country; there equality is imposed upon society by an all-powerful government. The genius of American politics consists in its ability to create the conditions of equal opportunity, of the equal chance for all to advance as far as their abilities allow them to go, under the conditions of free elections and free competition. That conception is challenged today at home and abroad by novel developments, unforeseen and unforeseeable by past generations. The most important of those new developments is the technological revolutions of recent times, of which the nuclear revolution is the most spectacular one.

The nuclear revolution, which I take here to be representative of all the others, led to a radical change in the distribution of power between the government and the people, by concentrating unprecedented power in the hands of the government, available for use at home and abroad. A hundred years ago, the physical violence at the disposal of the government was not radically different from the physical violence at the disposal of the people. The people had essentially the same kind of weapons at their disposal as the government, and when their patience was exhausted, they could attempt to overthrow the government by violent means. Whether or not they would prevail was a matter of numbers, discipline, morale, and leadership. In any event, the odds were not from the outset against the victory of the people. Popular revolution was an ever present possibility, and that possibility constituted a potent and at least implicitly recognized check upon the powers of the government. A wise government would go so far and no further for fear of provoking a popular revolution.

No government which controls the instruments of modern technology and can rely upon the loyalty of the armed forces need fear a popular revolution. It is not by accident that the last popular revolution occurred in a technologically backward country, Russia, in 1917. On the other hand, the so-called fascist revolutions in Italy and Germany were not revolutions but coups d'état. The fascist governments came into power by constitutional or quasi-constitutional means. They did not seize power by force of arms. Thus the technologically advanced nations are today threatened not by the people rising against them, but by the armed forces disobeying them. It is interesting to note that France, the nation which gave us in 1789 the classic example of a popular revolution, is also the nation which recently gave us the classic example of a government which governs not with the consent of the people but with the consent of the army. In France it was the army which decided who should govern, how far the government could go, what it could and what it could not do, and the army *Putsch*, the revolt of the generals, became the substitute for the parliamentary vote of lack of confidence.

This is a very significant development, whose potentialities exist everywhere. In all technologically advanced nations we are in the presence of an entirely new distribution of power within the state. In these nations, the armed forces occupy a key position because of their monopolistic possession of the most powerful instruments of violence. That this problem has not become acute in this country is due primarily to the strong tradition of civilian control of the armed forces. But, as President Eisenhower pointed out in his farewell address, this ascendancy of the military, especially when combined with industrial power, constitutes a threat to democratic institutions.

As nuclear power confronts American society with new problems domestically, so it does on the international scene. When I speak here of the availability of nuclear weapons, I am using the terms merely as a symbol of a revolution in warfare covering other weapons less frequently mentioned in public but no less destructive, such as bacteriological and chemical ones. The availability of nuclear weapons has caused the first real revolution in the structure of international relations. From the beginning of history to the end of World War II, that is to say, to the beginning of the nuclear age, there has always existed a rational relationship between violence as a means and the ends of foreign policy. Throughout history, a statesman would always calculate, and could calculate rationally, whether he could achieve his aims by peaceful means, that is, by diplomatic pressure, economic inducements, propaganda, and the like, or whether he had to resort to war. And if he resorted to war, his decision was arrived at by way of a rational calculation, which was no less rational for turning out to have been mistaken. Even Hitler, whose objectives were unlimited, acted in a rational way by committing all of the resources of Germany for this goal. For even when Germany lost her bid for world dominion, Germany had not lost everything; even a truncated Germany is again today one of the most powerful nations on earth.

This rational relationship between violence as a means and the ends of foreign policy has been radically altered by the introduction of nuclear weapons into the arsenal of foreign policy. Assume for a moment, and this is more than a mere hypothetical assumption, that a nuclear war were fought over the Western presence in Berlin or the Russian presence in Cuba. Most certainly the objective of such a war would be wiped off the face of the earth and, in all probability, the belligerents as well. A war which would destroy the very objective for which it was fought, together with the belligerents, is obviously an utterly irrational undertaking. Thus the availability of nuclear weapons has created an unprecedented situation which has rendered obsolete the traditional relationship between violence as a means and the ends of foreign policy.

It is one of the paradoxes of our situation that, by dint of this enormous increase in power, the government is no longer able to use its power as effectively as it did in times past. Let me demonstrate this paradox by the example of Cuba. Fifty or even twenty years ago, it would have been a simple operation to get rid of Castro by sending a regiment of marines to Cuba. Today, the United States, having much more material power than it ever had before in relation to Cuba, can no longer afford to use that power. The reason lies in the irrationality of nuclear power as an instrument of foreign policy. Implicit in the use of any force, however conventional and limited it may be initially, there is today, as John Foster Dulles clearly recognized, the possibility of escalation into all-out nuclear war. Thus a nation as powerful in terms of its material resources as the United States is much less able to commit its power to the support of its interests than it was when it had much less power.

Another paradox with which we have to come to terms in our theory and practice of government is the result of a fundamental misunderstanding of the nature of the American political legacy and, more particularly, of American democracy. Opposed to the Anglo-American conception of democracy as restraint upon the government is the French or Jacobin conception, which assumes that the rule of the majority is the ultimate standard for political thought and action. This conception has its roots in the political philosophy of Rousseau. In contrast, the American political tradition has always assumed that there exist certain objective standards for the judgment of political thought and action, which are independent of the will of the majority and by which the will of the majority itself must be judged. Consider as a case in point the institution of judicial review. The American political tradition assumes here the existence of what the constitutional theorists of the early nineteenth century called the "higher law," certain objective rules of conduct which were not made by man—you may consider in this context the reference of the Declaration of Independence to "the laws of nature and nature's god"—and which are not subject to change by the rule of changing majorities.

In order to assure that government policy conforms to the will of the people, we have come to understand American democracy more and more as the rule of the majority. However, in the process of this extension of the majority principle the influence of the people upon the government has drastically declined. This is the paradox of contemporary American democracy.

We have followed in the course of the twentieth century a tendency toward accepting step by step the French conception of democracy to the detriment of the Anglo-American tradition, that is to say, our own political legacy. This is most obvious in our reliance on public opinion polls as the ultimate standard of political judgment. Public opinion polls have become one of the major sources by which the government determines what kind of policy, domestic or international, it ought to pursue. This reliance upon public opinion polls is based upon the assumption that public opinion is a kind of datum of nature, something that pre-exists policy and toward which policy must be oriented. This is an erroneous conception.

Public opinion is created by somebody. The man in the street does not carry in his head a series of judgments about policy. He knows nothing or very little about political problems which do not affect his person directly; he follows in the formation of his own opinions the leadership of somebody. If it is not the government, or more particularly the President, who gives him that leadership, somebody else, that is, the opposition, will. Yet the opposition can criticize but is unable to substitute policies of its own for those the government has failed to provide. So the reliance on the part of the executive branch upon public opinion as the guide toward which public policy must be oriented, which has become for all practical purposes standard operating procedure since the end of World War II, constitutes a corruption of the political processes of democracy as they have been developed by the American political tradition. For this conception of the relationship between policy formation and public opinion leads of necessity to the abdication of governmental and, more particularly, presidential leadership.

The true order of things, which all great Presidents have recognized—in good measure we call them great because they have recognized it—consists in the President's giving the lead, educating the people, and forming a public opinion on behalf of his policies. If the President does not perform this function, nobody else will, and policy formation, the formation of new policies, goes by default; for it is left to an opposition, which in the nature of things is incapable of action, to fill the place which the President has vacated. Thus the restoration of this vital relationship between the executive branch and, more particularly, the President, on the one hand, and the people at large, on the other, is the first great practical task with which the reconsideration of the American political legacy must come to terms. For whatever tasks the American people must perform, whatever functions different branches of the government must fulfil, if the President does not perform his function as the educator of the people, as the creator of a public opinion supporting his policies, all relations within the American political system will be in disorder; the whole dynamics of American politics will be out of joint.

Looking, as it were, at the other side of the political fence, the people's side, we discover the true import of this domestic paradox of contemporary American politics. For, on the one hand, the trend toward majority rule, toward the majoritarian conception of democracy, such as the deference to public opinion, makes the people at large more powerful than they ever were before. But, on the other hand, as a matter of fact, the influence of the people at large upon the formation of policy today is much inferior to that which existed in times past. Take the great vital decisions which our government must make in the field of military and foreign policy and try to assess the influence of the popular will upon them. The part which the will of the people played, for instance, in the decision which our government made in 1961 to resume atmospheric nuclear tests was minimal. The facts of the situation, the arguments in favor of the decision to resume atmospheric nuclear tests were presented to the people at the very moment the President made public his decision to resume those tests. This decision was not preceded by democratic discussion. The American people were confronted with an accomplished fact and with a rational case in favor of that fact. The American people at large had no influence upon the decision. If you examine any other of the great issues, domestic or international, which confront America today, you will find that public participation in those decisions is minimal, if it exists at all, in spite of the general trend toward deferring to public opinion and toward substituting the majoritarian conception of democracy for the Anglo-American one.

The reason for this decline in democratic participation in, and in the influence of the people at large upon, the formation of policy is to be found in good measure in the nature of the issues which are before the American people today. Let us consider two examples, one taken from the domestic field, the other from the field of military and foreign policy.

A hundred years ago, the issue of race relations in the United States presented itself as the issue of abolitionism versus slavery. Every individual could make up his mind on the basis of his interests or moral and religious preference and choose sides accordingly; he was either in favor of or against the abolition of slavery, and this was all there was to it.

Today the same issue presents itself in the form of racial integration on all levels of social interaction. While it is simple to give a positive or negative answer to the question of integration on moral and rational grounds, the implementation of the answer in practice raises a host of issues of great complexity. These issues cannot be disposed of by simple —positive or negative—answers. They will be settled by a series of drawn-out and painful and sometimes inconclusive social experiences. A vote will not settle these issues; it will only provide the legal and moral precondition for their solution by other means.

Take as an instance from military and foreign policy the issue of banning atomic tests, a relatively simple issue as issues in that field go. Are you in favor of it or are you against it? Arguing from your emotions, the answer is simple, one way or the other. But when you consider the technical aspects, the bearing, for instance, of the continuation or cessation of atomic tests upon the balance of military power, you are confronted with a series of highly complex and, more particularly, unpredictable technological hypotheses upon which no individual citizen, expert or not, can really have a completely rational judgment. We all reason in such a case from hunches, more or less informed, yet inevitably devoid of that black-and-white quality in contemplation of which the man in the street fashions his political judgment.

And so it comes to pass that in the face of these complex issues, many of which are furthermore far removed from the day-by-day experiences of the individual, the man in the street simply throws up his hands, retreats into his private sphere, votes according to his tradition or emotional preferences, but no longer participates fully in the public discussion of vital issues. Paradoxically, the triumph of the majority principle goes hand in hand with the atrophy of the democratic process.

Thus the novel factors which face us in our domestic and international life require a reformulation of the basic principles of the American political tradition in the light of the new conditions of the contemporary world. That reformulation and modernization will occur not in the study of a professor where theories are spun, but in the market place where the political battles are fought out. The American political tradition will be renewed through the interplay of political forces, guided by individuals who are aware of the issue, that is, the nature of the American political tradition and the need for its reformulation and adaptation to modern conditions. What is necessary today is, then, not so much a theoretical outline, an abstract recipe, but rather an awareness of the nature of the problem and of the intellectual categories to be brought to bear upon the political issues of the day.